A STRAIGHTFORWARD GUIDE
TO
THE RIGHTS OF THE PRIVATE
TENANT

ROGER SPROSTON

STRAIGHTFORWARD PUBLISHING
WWW.STRAIGHTFORWARDCO.CO.UK

Straightforward Publishing

© Straightforward Publishing 2017

All rights reserved. No part of this publication may be reproduced in a retrieval system or transmitted by any means, electronic or mechanical, photocopying or otherwise, without the prior permission of the copyright holder.

ISBN

978-1-84716-714-9

Printed by 4edge Press www.4edge.co.uk

Cover design by Bookworks Islington

The information in this book was correct at the time of going to print. The author and publishers cannot be held liable for any errors or omissions within or for any changes in law since publication.

CONTENTS

3

****

INTRODUCTION

This latest edition of A Straightforward Guide to the Rights of the Private Tenant, 2017, substantially updates the previous edition by introducing more detailed information concerning the law, landlords obligations and tenants rights and obligations. It also includes a brief section on leaseholders.

More and more people, in the next few years, due to factors such as inability to access finance to purchase a house, due to high costs of housing, changes in the housing benefit system and homelessness legislation will become reliant on the private sector. The private sector is rapidly expanding, because of a combination of these factors and rents are on the increase, in particular in London and the South East. In their recent report, Generation Rent, A Society Divided the Halifax states that the private rented sector is now at its highest level since the early 1990's. In 2017-2018 there are an estimated 22 million households in England and Wales living in private accommodation. With no prospect of buying, more and more people will populate the private market over the coming years. Correspondingly, many more people have become landlords, particularly since 1988, and many more are set to become landlords, although the banks and government are making it that much harder through economic sanctions. It is the case, unfortunately, that this expansion introduces a lot of inexperienced people into the field. If an agent is used in the letting of property then there is (usually) no problem, although that is not a given. However, when the property is directly managed then issues can arise that can lead to conflict.

The aim of this book is to ensure that all are clear about the law and practice of letting and residing in, private sector tenanted property. The book covers the finding of a property, the law, detailed information on specific tenancies, payments of rent and benefits and repairing obligations. Issues such as unlawful eviction and harassment are covered, as are public sector tenancies plus tenancies in Scotland. There is a section on the processes involved in regaining possession of a home for breach of tenancy.

The various notices used when going to court, and other forms associated with landlord and tenant can be obtained from the county courts. accessed and all the necessary forms required in relation to housing matters can be downloaded from:

www.gov.uk/government/organisations/hm-courts-and-tribunals-servicebe The court service website also gives a lot of valuable information in relation to housing.

The main aim of this book is to inform the would-be tenant, or the landlord, about their rights and obligations and covers all areas in depth. It is to be hoped that an invaluable insight is gained and that both landlord and tenant can operate more effectively.

Roger Sproston
2017

Ch. 1

Finding a Property

Checking landlords

With so many landlords about, it is odds on that a percentage of them will be sub-standard, not up to the job of providing a good service. A new site, Rental Raters, www.rentalraters.com allows you to search and find out what rating your landlord has been given in terms of overall efficiency and honesty. Your landlord may not be on this site but it is worth checking.

Letting Agents

When looking for a property, there are obvious advantages to using a reputable agent (emphasize reputable): they are likely to be experienced, can provide you with a tenancy agreement and they can provide a service after the property is let. It is important for a tenant to know that there will be a proper relationship between him/her and the landlord after moving in. Managing agents will provide this link.

Agents will typically look after the following:

- Take up references/sign tenancy/take deposit.
- Carry out the mandatory checks of passports and residency permits to identify if a potential tenant has the right to reside in the UK. These checks have to be carried out by all landlords or their agents on every new tenant age 18 or over

and applied to all landlords, including those who take in lodgers and landlords and tenants who sublet property. (see below)

- Transfer the utility bills and the council tax into the name of the tenant.
- Pay for repairs, although an agent will only normally do this if rent is being paid directly to them and they can make appropriate deductions.
- Chase rent arrears
- Serve prescribed documentation at the outset of the tenancy, such as the Department for Communities and Local Government's publication "How to rent: the checklist for renting in England" (a pdf copy suffices) which may be obtained from www.gov.uk/government/publications/how-torent).
- Provide an Energy Performance Certificate (Reg 6(5), The Energy Performance of Buildings (England and Wales) Regulations 2012); and a gas safety certificate (Reg 36(6)(a), The Gas Safety (Installation and Use) Regulations 1998)
- Visit the property at regular intervals and check that the tenants are not causing any damage.
- Deal with neighbor complaints
- Bank rental receipts if the landlord is abroad
- Deal with housing benefit departments if necessary. The extent to which agents actually do all of the above really depends on the caliber of the agent. It also depends on the type of agreement the landlord has with the agent.

Right to rent immigration checks
How landlords check you have the right to rent

Before you can rent a home in England, a landlord or letting agent must check your immigration status and that of anyone aged 18 or over who'll be living with you. They'll ask to see your passport or other official documents that prove your immigration status. They must take copies of the documents and keep the copies safe. Current or expired passports are acceptable documents for British, Irish and EU citizens.

If you are a British or Irish citizen without a passport, your birth certificate plus another accepted proof of identity should be enough. For a full list of acceptable documents, see Gov.uk: Right to rent documents check. A landlord or letting agent is allowed to charge you a fee for right to rent checks.

Checks if you don't have documents

A check can be done even if the Home Office has your original documents because of an ongoing immigration application or appeal. The landlord or letting agent can ask for a Home Office right to rent check. They'll need your Home Office reference number and should get a response within 2 days.

When checks are needed for private tenants

Right to rent checks must be done before you start a private tenancy in England. The checks apply to verbal and written agreements. Checks are needed for tenancies that started from:

- 1 February 2016 anywhere in England

- 1   December   2014   in Birmingham,   Dudley, Sandwell, Walsall and Wolverhampton

A check isn't needed if you became a tenant before these dates and your landlord renews your agreement. A landlord or letting agent can't rent you the place if you can't show you have the right to rent. Your landlord must make sure that any other adults living in the property have the right to rent, so must check their immigration status too. Your landlord could be fined or imprisoned if they don't do this.

Checks aren't needed for guests in your home. A guest includes someone whose main home is somewhere else or who doesn't pay you rent. Contributions towards food and costs such as gas and electricity don't count as rent. Immigration checks aren't needed for children aged under 18, but landlords should check they are aged under 18.

Right to rent checks for lodgers

Right to rent checks are needed for lodgers. The checks apply to people renting a room from home-owners, private tenants, council tenants or housing association tenants. Right to rent checks are needed if a lodger moves in from:

- 1 February 2016 anywhere in England
- 1   December   2014   in Birmingham,   Dudley, Sandwell, Walsall and Wolverhampton

A check isn't needed if you became a lodger before these dates and your landlord renews your agreement.

Checks if you have a time limited right to rent

If a right to rent check showed there's a time limit on your permission to stay in the UK, your landlord must do a follow-up check. The deadline for this is the latest of these dates:

- 12 months after the last check
- the date your permission to stay in the UK runs out
- the expiry date of passport or other document that shows your right to be in the UK

The check can be done up to 28 days before the deadline. Your landlord must tell the Home Office if a follow up check shows you no longer have the right to rent.

Eviction if you don't have the right to rent

A landlord must take reasonable steps to evict tenants or lodgers if:

- the Home Office sends them a notice that says someone living in their household doesn't have the right to rent
- a follow up check shows you no longer have the right to rent

Your landlord is allowed time to come to an agreement with you about when you will move out. It's considered reasonable, for example, for you to leave at the end of your tenancy's fixed term if there are 3 months or less left to run.

Eviction if no-one in your home has the right to rent
Special rules apply if:

- you are a single person household and you don't have the right to rent
- you live with other adults and none of you have the right to rent

If you don't reach an agreement about when you will move out, your landlord can give you 28 days' notice to leave. The notice must be on a special form with a copy of the Home Office notice attached. If you stay past the 28 day deadline, your landlord can evict you (they don't need a court order but shouldn't use force) or they can ask bailiffs from the High Court to do so. If you are a lodger and you don't have the right to rent, your landlord may only have to give you reasonable notice to leave.

Eviction if someone in your home has the right to rent
If you're in a household that includes two or more adults, your landlord must take action to end the tenancy if any of you don't have the right to rent. It's reasonable for a landlord to:

- agree to rent to adults who do have a right to rent if anyone without the right to rent has moved out
- take steps to evict everyone in your household, including children and those who do have the right to rent.

Your landlord must follow the correct legal process for eviction. A court order is usually needed.

Check if you have the right to rent
You have the right to rent if you are:

- British
- a citizen of a country in the EU or EEA
- a citizen of another country with no time limits on your permission to live in the UK (such as indefinite leave to remain)

You can have a time-limited right to rent if there's a time limit on your permission to stay in the UK. This is likely if you have a visa:

- for work
- to study
- as a husband, wife or civil partner of someone settled in the UK

The time-limited right to rent also applies if you have humanitarian protection, limited leave or discretionary leave to remain. See Gov.uk to check who has the right to rent.

Beware! There are many so-called rental agencies, which have sprung up since the last property recession in the 1990's and also the advent of "Buy to Let". These agents are not professional, do not know a thing about property management, are shady and should be avoided like the plague. Many of them will try to charge an upfront fee, sometimes amounting to £700 (the average is £300) for processing documents. they may also try to levy a 'reservation fee'. A good lettings agent will charge no fee at all, as they receive fees from landlords when letting the property.

(It was announced in the Autumn 2016 statement by the Chancellor that there is the intention to abolish fees charged by letting agents. Currently, this is 'out for consultation'. However, whether this ever becomes law is another matter).

It is most important to shop around and seek a reputable agent. In a climate of shortage of good private rented stock, where there is competition, in places such as London in particular, rogue 'agents' carry out scams such as letting non-existent properties or letting the same property twice. It is very wise to have your wits about you and ensure that you are dealing with honest, reputable agents.

Redress schemes
An amendment to the Enterprise and Regulatory Reform Act 2013 enabled the Government to require agents to sign up to a redress scheme. The Redress Scheme for Lettings Agency Work and Property Management Work (Requirement to Belong to a Scheme etc) (England) Order 2014 made membership of a scheme a legal requirement with effect from 1 October 2014. The Government also amended the Consumer Rights Act 2015 to require letting agents to publish a full tariff of their fees. If you intend to use an agent to find a property then ensure that it is signed up to a redress scheme. One such scheme is The Property Ombudsman Scheme. references of potential tenants.

How do you tell if a letting agent is a TPO registered letting agent?

All agents must display the TPO logo on windows, advertising and stationery. If you need help in finding an agent you can contact the Ombudsman's office or look at the TPO website www.tpos.co.uk. All agents are required to display copies of the TPO Consumer Guide in their office and make copies available, free of charge, on request.

Online lettings agents

The rise of online lettings agents has been rapid and they now account for 3.5% of the market. The attractions are obvious, the costs.

One of the biggest online property agents, EasyProperty.com offers 'pick and mix' services for landlords and tenants, ranging from £10 a week for adverts on Right Move, Prime Location and Zoopla to 3% commission for full property management. For tenant finding with all the frills, such as hosted viewings and professional photos to check-in the total bill would be £445. This equates to less than half the commission charged by high-street agents. Another agent, Purplebricks.com is also very competitive. However, there can be drawbacks.

The main drawback is accessibility. If you have your contract with a local agent, they will be there when you want them. Online tends to be one step removed. You are strongly advised to consider what it is you want before entering into any deal with an online agent.

Advertisements

The classified advertisement section of local papers is a good place to seek a property, local papers are obviously cheaper than the nationals such as the Evening Standard in London or the broadsheets such as the Guardian. The type of newspaper you look in will largely reflect what type of property you are looking for. An advert in the pages of the Times would indicate that the landlord is looking for a well-heeled professional and this would be reflected in the type of property that is to let.

Company lets

Where the tenant is a company rather than an individual, the tenancy agreement will be similar to an assured shorthold, but will not be bound by the six-month rule (see chapter 7 for details of assured shorthold tenancies). Company lets can be from any length of time, from a week to several years, or as long as you like. The major difference between contracts and standard assured shorthold agreements is that the contract will be tailored to individual needs, and the agreement is bound by the provisions of contract law. Company tenancies are bound by the provisions of contract law and not by the 1988 Housing Act. Note: if you are a company and you are looking for a property to rent or let you must use a letting agent or solicitor. The advantages of a landlord letting to a company are:

A company or embassy has no security of tenure and therefore cannot be a sitting tenant. A company cannot seek to reduce the rent by statutory interventions. Rental payments are often made quarterly or six monthly in advance.

The financial status of a company is usually more secure than that of an individual. Company tenants often require long-term lets to accommodate staff relocating on contracts of between one and five years.

The main disadvantages of company lets are:
A company tenancy can only be to a bona fide company or embassy, not to a private individual.

A tenancy to a partnership would not count as a company let and may have some security of tenure.

If the tenant is a foreign government, the diplomatic status of the occupant must be ascertained, as the courts cannot enforce breaches of contract with somebody who possesses diplomatic immunity.
A tenancy to a foreign company not registered in the U.K may prove time consuming and costly if it becomes necessary to pursue claims for unpaid rent or damage through foreign courts.

Short lets
Although company lets can be of any length, it is becoming increasingly popular for companies to rent flats from private landlords on short lets.

A short let is any let of less than six months. But here, it is essential to check the rules with any borough concerned. Some boroughs will not allow lets for less than three months, as they do not want to encourage transient people in the neighborhood.

Generally speaking, short lets are only applicable in large cities where there is a substantial shifting population. Business executives on temporary relocation, actors and others involved in television production or film work, contract workers and visiting academics are examples of people who might require a short let.

From a landlord's point of view, short lets are an excellent idea if you have to vacate your own home for seven or eight months, say, and do not want to leave it empty for that time. Short let tenants provide useful extra income as well as keeping an eye on the place.

Short let tenants are, usually, from a landlord's point of view, excellent blue-chip occupants. They are busy professionals, high earners, out all day and used to high standards. As the rent is paid by the company there is no worry for the landlord on this score either.

A major plus of short lets is that they command between 20-50% more rent than the optimum market rent for that type of property. The one downside of short lets is that no agency can guarantee permanent occupancy.

Letting through Airbnb

Over the last few years, landlords have increasingly turned to companies like Airbnb to let their properties. What started out as a good concept has, as usual been ruined by those looking for a quick return, Airbnb started out as a web based company offering an alternative to hotels, particularly in the overpriced capitals of the world. Landlords now see that there is a profit to be made by allowing a succession of short term tenants to stay in their properties.

However, problems have arisen and the courts have found that for landlords with leasehold property to allow their properties to be used by a succession of short term tenants is actually a breach of the lease. If you are a tenant and intend using sites such as Airbnb make sure that the let is safe and secure and that you are not entering into a situation where you may find yourself homeless.

Student lets

Many letting agencies will not consider students and a lot of landlords similarly are not keen. There is the perception that students will not look after a home and tend to live a lifestyle guaranteed to increase the wear and tear on a property. However, if handled correctly, student lets can be profitable. Students quite often want property for only eight or nine months, but agencies that deal with students make them sign for a whole year. Rent is guaranteed by confirmation that the student is a genuine student with references from parents, who act as guarantors.

If you are a student, you should locate an agency that specializes in student lets or look in the local newspaper which will advertise houses or flats, usually with a room rental rate.

The DSS and housing benefit

Until recently, very few letting agencies or landlords would touch DSS or housing benefit tenants. However, as with student lets, there is another side of the coin. Times are changing and landlords are seeing a new business opportunity with more reliance by local authorities and housing associations, on the private rented sector.

Quite often it is essential for a tenant on HB to have a guarantor, usually a homeowner, before signing a tenancy. Then it is up to the machinations of the benefit system to ensure that the landlord receives rent. The rent is assessed by a benefit officer, with the rent estimated usually at market price. There are rent levels set for each area that the benefit officer will not go above. A deposit is paid normally and rent is paid, in some cases, direct to the landlord. We will be discussing benefits later on in the book.

Holiday lets

Before the Housing Act 1988 became law, many landlords advertised their properties as holiday lets to bypass the rules regarding security of tenure. Strictly speaking, a holiday let is a property let for no more than a month to any one tenant. If the same tenant renews for another month then the landlord is breaking the law. Nowadays, holiday lets must be just that-let for a genuine holiday.

Holiday lets are not covered by the Housing Act. The contract is finalized by exchange of letters with the tenant where they place a deposit and the owner confirms the booking. If the let is not for a genuine holiday you may have problems in evicting the tenant, as the whole point of a holiday let is that it is for no more than a fixed period of a month.

Generally speaking, certain services must be provided for the let to be deemed a holiday let. Cleaning services and changes of bed linen are essential. The amount paid by the holidaymaker will usually include utilities but would exclude use of the telephone, fax machine etc.

Bedsits

Bedsitting rooms are usually difficult to let and can cause problems for tenants as well as landlords. However, they are usually plentiful, as are studios. Make sure that you have a clear idea of what facilities are available and what the rent includes, i.e. does it include water or council tax.

Viewing a property-The tenant

Once you have found a property, the next stage is to make arrangements for a viewing. It is a good idea to make all appointments on the same day in order to avoid wasting time. If you decide on a likely property, the landlord will wish to take up references, if an agency is not being used. This will normally be a previous landlord's reference and also a bank reference. Only when these have been received and it is established that the person(s) are safe will the letting go ahead. No keys will be handed over until the cheque has been cleared and the landlord is in receipt of a month's rent and a month's deposit.

Deposits
Tenancy Deposit Protection Scheme

The Tenancy Deposit Protection Scheme was introduced to protect all deposits paid to landlords after 6th April 2007. After this date, landlords and/or agents must use a government authorised scheme to protect deposits. The Deregulation Act 2015 has extended this requirement to all landlords to ensure that deposits paid before this date are also registered. The need for such a scheme has arisen because of the historical problem with deposits and the abuse of deposits by landlords. The scheme works as follows:

Moving into a property

At the beginning of a new tenancy agreement, the tenant will pay a deposit to the landlord or agent as usual.

Prescribed Information must be served on the tenant and on any relevant person within the period of 30 days from and including the date the landlord (or someone acting on the landlord's behalf) receives a deposit in relation to an assured shorthold tenancy, irrespective of whether or not the funds have cleared.

A "relevant person" is a person, company or organisation who, in accordance with arrangements made with the tenant, paid the deposit on behalf of the tenant e.g. a local authority, employer, parent or guarantor. Members are advised to establish, when a tenant applies for a tenancy, whether a deposit has been (or will be) paid by someone other than the tenant, because the member will have to serve Prescribed Information on such a person.

The Deregulation Act 2015 has led to some important changes in respect of Prescribed Information and has led to this becoming a less onerous obligation on landlords.

- Prescribed Information should be served each time there is a new AST within 30 days of a new AST being created;

- If the tenancy rolls over into a new fixed term AST or a statutory periodic tenancy there is no need to re-issue the Prescribed Information as long as:

- The deposit was properly protected and Prescribed Information served at the start of the original tenancy;

- The property let remains the same;

- The tenant(s) remain the same;

- The landlord(s) remain the same;

- The deposit protection scheme used remains the same.

- In the event that any of the above conditions do not apply the deposit needs to be protected and the Prescribed Information served within 30 days of the tenancy change.

Failure to serve the Prescribed Information within the correct timescale will be a breach of the Housing Act 2004 and could expose the landlord and/or deposit holder to legal action for compensation by the tenant and/or the relevant person.

The Prescribed Information may be attached to the tenancy agreement, or served as a stand-alone document. The Prescribed Information includes the scheme leaflet What is the Tenancy Deposit Scheme? Both landlord or agent and tenant must sign the last page of the Prescribed Information.

There are three tenancy deposit schemes that a landlord can opt for:

Tenancy Deposit Solutions Ltd
www.mydeosits.co.uk
info@mydeposits.co.uk

The Tenancy Deposit Scheme
www.tds.gb.com
0845 226 7837

The Deposit Protection Service
www.depositprotection.com
0870 707 1 707

The schemes above fall into two categories, insurance based schemes and custodial schemes.

Custodial Scheme
The tenant pays the deposit to the landlord

- The landlord pays the deposit into the scheme
- Within 30 days of receiving the deposit, the landlord must give the tenant prescribed information
- A the end of the tenancy, if the landlord and tenant have agreed how much of the deposit is to be returned, they will tell the scheme which returns the deposit, divided in the way agreed by the parties.
- If there is a dispute, the scheme will hold the disputed amount until the dispute resolution service or courts decide what is fair

The interest accrued by deposits in the scheme will be used to pay for the running of the scheme and any surplus will be used to offer interest to the tenant, or landlord if the tenant isn't entitled to it.

Insurance based schemes

- The tenant pays the deposit to the landlord
- The landlord retains the deposit and pays a premium to the insurer (this is the key difference between the two schemes)
- Within 30 days of receiving a deposit the landlord must give the tenant prescribed information.
- At the end of the tenancy if the landlord and tenant agree how the deposit is to be divided or otherwise then the landlord will return the amount agreed
- If there is a dispute, the landlord must hand over the disputed amount to the scheme for safekeeping until the dispute is resolved

If for any reason the landlord fails to comply, the insurance arrangements will ensure the return of the deposit to the tenant if they are entitled to it. If a landlord or agent hasn't protected a deposit with one of the above then the tenant can apply to the local county court for an order for the landlord either to protect the deposit or repay it.

Rental guarantees

The landlord will always obtain a guarantor if there is any potential uncertainty as to payment of rent. One example is where the tenant is on benefits. The guarantor will be expected to assume responsibility for the rent if the tenant ceases to pay at any time during the term of the tenancy.

In chapter two we will explore the legal framework governing residential lettings.

Ch. 2

The Law in a Nutshell

Explaining the law

As a tenant, or potential tenant, it is very important to understand the rights and obligations of both yourself and your landlord, exactly what can and what cannot be done once the tenancy agreement has been signed and you have moved into the property.

Some landlords think they can do exactly as they please, because the property belongs to them. Some tenants do not know any differently and therefore the landlord can, and often does, get away with breaking the law. However there is a very strong legal framework governing the relationship between landlord and tenant and it is important that you have a grasp of the key principles of the law.

In order to fully understand the law we should begin by looking at the main types of relationship between people and their homes.

The freehold and the lease

In law, there are two main types of ownership and occupation of property. These are: freehold and leasehold. These arrangements are very old indeed. In the section dealing with the relationship between leaseholder and freeholder, towards the end of this book, we will be discussing leasehold and freehold in more depth.

Freehold

If a person owns their property outright (usually with a mortgage) then they are a freeholder. The only claims to ownership over and above their own might be those of the building society or the bank, which lent them the money to buy the property. They will re-possess the property if the mortgage payments are not kept up with.

In certain situations though, the local authority (council) for an area can affect a person's right to do what they please with their home even if they are a freeholder. This will occur when planning powers are exercised, for example, in order to prevent the carrying out of alterations without consent.

The local authority for your area has many powers and we will be referring to these regularly.

Leasehold

If a person lives in a property owned by someone else and has a written agreement allowing them to occupy the flat or house for a period of time I.e., giving them permission to live in that property, then they will, in the main, have a lease and either be a leaseholder or a tenant of a landlord.

The main principle of a lease is that a person has been given permission by someone else to live in his or her property for a period of time. The person giving permission could be either the freeholder or another leaseholder. The tenancy agreement is one type of lease. If you have signed a tenancy agreement then you will have been given permission by a person to live in their property for a period of time.

The position of the tenant

The tenant will usually have an agreement for a shorter period of time than the typical leaseholder. Whereas the leaseholder will, for example, have an agreement for ninety-nine years, the tenant will have an agreement, which either runs from week to week or month to month (periodic tenancy) or is for a fixed term, for example, six-months or one-year.

These arrangements are the most common types of agreement between the private landlord and tenant.

The agreement itself will state whether it is a fixed term or periodic tenancy. If an agreement has not been issued it will be assumed to be a fixed-term tenancy.

Both periodic and fixed term tenants will usually pay a sum of rent regularly to a landlord in return for permission to live in the property (more about rent and service charges later)

The tenancy agreement

The tenancy agreement is the usual arrangement under which one person will live in a property owned by another. Before a tenant moves into a property he/she will have to sign a tenancy agreement drawn up by a landlord or landlord's agent. *A tenancy agreement is a contract between landlord and tenant.* It is important to realize that when you sign a tenancy agreement, you have signed a contract with another person, which governs the way in which you will live in their property.

The contract

Typically, any tenancy agreement will show the name and address of the landlord and will state the names of the tenant(s). The type of tenancy agreement that is signed should be clearly indicated. This could be, for example, a Rent Act protected tenancy, an assured tenancy or an assured shorthold tenancy. In the main, in the private sector, the agreement will be an assured shorthold.

Date of commencement of tenancy and rent payable

The date the tenancy began and the duration (fixed term or periodic) plus the amount of rent payable should be clearly shown, along with who is responsible for any other charges, such as water rates, council tax etc, and a description of the property you are living in.

In addition to the rent that must be paid there should be a clear indication of when a rent increase can be expected. This information is sometimes shown in other conditions of tenancy, which should be given to the tenant when they move into their home. The conditions of tenancy will set out landlords and tenants rights and obligations.

Services provided under the tenancy and service of notice

If services are provided, i.e., if a service charge is payable, this should be indicated in the agreement. The tenancy agreement should indicate clearly the address to which notices on the landlord can be served by the tenant, for example, because of repair problems or notice of leaving the property. The landlord has a legal requirement to indicate this.

Tenants obligations

The tenancy agreement will either be a basic document with the above information or will be more comprehensive. Either way, there will be a section beginning "the tenant agrees." Here the tenant will agree to move into the property, pay rent, use the property as an only home, not cause a nuisance to others, take responsibility for certain internal repairs, not sublet the property, i.e., create another tenancy, and various other things depending on the property. (The government is, at the moment, actively considering allowing tenants to sublet). It is important that when looking at a tenancy agreement it complies with legislation.

Landlords obligations

There should also be another section "the landlord agrees". Here, the landlord is contracting with the tenant to allow quiet enjoyment of the property. The landlord's repairing responsibilities are also usually outlined.

Ending a tenancy

Finally, there should be a section entitled "ending the tenancy" which will outline the ways in which landlord and tenant can end the agreement. The landlord can only end a fixed term assured shorthold tenancy by issuing a s21 notice (so called because it arises out of section 21 of the Housing Act 1988, as amended) two months prior to the end of the tenancy. Many landlords issued this notice at the outset of the tenancy. However, the Deregulation Act 2015 has effectively stopped this practice and states that the landlord cannot now service the notice until the tenant has been in occupation for at least four months. The tenant, after the expiry of the fixed term, can give one months notice to leave. One more point worth noting is that, if the landlord issues notice, in the required format, by text or email this is likely to be accepted as valid notice.

The landlord must serve a notice by using Form 6A for all tenancies created on or after October 1st 2015. This form must be used for all ASTs created on or after 1 October 2015 except for statutory periodic tenancies which have come into being on or after 1 October 2015 at the end of fixed term ASTs created before 1 October 2015.

See appendix for a sample Form 6A.

It is also in this section of the tenancy that the landlord should make reference to the "grounds for possession". Grounds for possession are circumstances where the landlord will apply to court for possession of his/her property. Some of these grounds relate to what is in the tenancy, i.e., the responsibility to pay rent and to not cause a nuisance. Other grounds do not relate to the contents of the tenancy directly, but more to the law governing that particular tenancy. The grounds for possession are very important, as they are used in any court case brought against the tenant. Unfortunately, they are not always indicated in the tenancy agreement. As they are so important they are summarized later on in the next chapter.

It must be said at this point that many residential tenancies are very light on spelling out landlord's responsibilities. For example, repairing responsibilities are landlords obligations under law. This book deals with these obligations, and also other important areas.

However, many landlords will seek to use only the most basic document in order to conceal legal obligations.

This is one of the main reasons for this book. It is essential that those who intend to let property for profit are able to manage professionally and set high standards as a private landlord. This is because the sector has been beset by rogues in the past. Correspondingly, as a tenant you need to know your rights very clearly and need to know how to enforce them.

The responsibility of the landlord to provide a rent book

If the tenant is a weekly periodic tenant the landlord must provide him/her with a rent book and commits a criminal offence if he/she does not do so. This is outlined in the Landlord and Tenant Act 1985 sections 4 - 7. Under this Act any tenant can ask in writing the name and address of the landlord. The landlord must reply within twenty-one days of asking. As most tenancies nowadays are fixed term assured shortholds then it is not strictly necessary to provide a tenant with a rent book.. However, for the purposes of efficiency, and your own records, it is always useful to have a rent book and sign it each time rent is collected or a standing order is paid.

Overcrowding

It is important to understand, when signing a tenancy agreement, that it is not permitted to allow the premises to become overcrowded, i.e., to allow more people than was originally intended, (which is outlined in the agreement) to live in the property. If a tenant does, then the landlord can take action to evict.

Different types of tenancy agreement

The protected tenancy - the meaning of the term

As a basic guide, if a person is a private tenant and signed their current agreement with a landlord before 15th January 1989 then they will, in most cases, be a protected tenant with all the rights relating to protection of tenure, which are considerable. Protection is provided under the 1977 Rent Act.

In practice, there are not many protected tenancies left and the tenant will usually be signing an assured shorthold tenancy.

The assured shorthold tenancy - what it means

If the tenant entered into an agreement with a landlord after 15th January 1989 then they will, in most cases, be an assured tenant. We will discuss assured tenancies in more depth in chapter three. In brief, there are various types of assured tenancy. The assured shorthold is usually a fixed term version of the assured tenancy and enables the landlord to recover their property after six months and to vary the rent after this time. *It is this tenancy that a private tenant will be signing.*

Other types of agreement

In addition to the above tenancy agreements, there are other types of agreement sometimes used in privately rented property. One of these is the company let, as we discussed in the last chapter, and another is the license agreement. The person signing such an agreement is called a licensee. Licenses will only apply in special circumstances where the licensee cannot be given sole occupation of his home and therefore can only stay for a short period with minimum rights.

Ch. 3

More About Assured Tenants

The assured tenant

As we discussed in Chapter two, all tenancies, (with the exceptions detailed entered into after 15th January 1989), are known as assured tenancies. An assured shorthold, which is the most common form of tenancy used by the landlord nowadays, is one type of assured tenancy, and is for a fixed term of six months minimum and can be brought to an end with two months notice by serving a section 21 (of the Housing Act 1988) notice.

For Assured shorthold tenancies beginning after October 1st 2015, a Form 6A must be used. it is possible to use form 6A for tenancies issued before that date although not necessary

As stated earlier, as a result of the passage of the 2015 Deregulation Act, the landlord cannot serve the notice until the tenant has been in occupation for four months (at least).

It is important to note that all tenancies signed after February 1997 are assured shorthold agreements unless otherwise stated.

Assured tenancies are governed by the 1988 Housing Act, as amended by the 1996 Housing Act. It is to these Acts, or outlines of the Acts that the tenant must refer when intending to sign a tenancy for a residential property. For a tenancy to be assured, three conditions must be fulfilled:

1. The premises must be a dwelling house. This basically means any premises which can be lived in. Business premises will normally fall outside this interpretation.
2. There must exist a particular relationship between landlord and tenant. In other words there must exist a tenancy agreement. For example, a license to occupy, as in the case of students, or accommodation occupied as a result of work, cannot be seen as a tenancy. Following on from this, the accommodation must be let as a single unit. The tenant, who must be an individual, must normally be able to sleep, cook and eat in the accommodation. Sharing of bathroom facilities will not prevent a tenancy being an assured tenancy but shared cooking or other facilities, such as a living room, will.
3. The third requirement for an assured tenancy is that the tenant must occupy the dwelling as his or her only or principal home. In situations involving joint tenants at least one of them must occupy.

Tenancies that are not assured

A tenancy agreement will not be assured if one of the following conditions applies:

-   The tenancy or the contract was entered into before 15th January 1989;

- If no rent is payable or if only a low rent amounting to less than two thirds of the present ratable value of the property is payable;
- If the premises are let for business purposes or for mixed residential and business purposes;
- If part of the dwelling house is licensed for the sale of liquor for consumption on the premises. This does not include the publican who lets out a flat;
- If the dwelling house is let with more than two acres of agricultural land;
- If the dwelling house is part of an agricultural holding and is occupied in relation to carrying out work on the holding;
- If the premises are let by a specified institution to students, i.e., halls of residence;
- If the premises are let for the purpose of a holiday;
- Where there is a resident landlord, e.g., in the case where the landlord has let one of his rooms but continues to live in the house;
- If the landlord is the Crown (the monarchy) or a government department. Certain lettings by the Crown are capable of being assured, such as some lettings by the Crown Estate Commissioners;
- If the landlord is a local authority, a fully mutual housing association (this is where you have to be a shareholder to be a tenant) a newly created Housing Action Trust or any similar body listed in the 1988 Housing Act.

- If the letting is transitional such as a tenancy continuing in its original form until phased out, such as:
- A protected tenancy under the 1977 Rent Act;
- Secure tenancy granted before 1st January 1989, e.g., from a local authority or housing association. These tenancies are governed by the 1985 Housing Act).

The Assured Shorthold tenancy

The assured shorthold tenancy as we have seen, is the most common form of tenancy used in the private sector. The main principle of the assured shorthold tenancy is that it is issued for a period of six months minimum and can be brought to an end by the landlord serving two months notice on the tenant. At the end of the six-month period the tenant, if given two months prior notice, must leave. If the tenant refuses to leave then the landlord can use a special 'fast track' procedure to get him/her out.

Any property let on an assured tenancy can be let on an assured shorthold, providing the following three conditions are met:

- The tenancy must be for a fixed term of not less than six months.
- The agreement cannot contain powers which enable the landlord to end the tenancy before six months. This does not include the right of the landlord to enforce the grounds for possession, which will be approximately the same as those for the assured tenancy (see below).

- A notice requiring possession at the end of the term is served two months before that date.
- A notice must be served before any rent increase giving one months clear notice and providing details of the rent increase.

If the landlord wishes to get possession of his/her property, in this case before the expiry of the contractual term, the landlord has to gain a court order. A notice of seeking possession must be served, giving fourteen days notice and following similar grounds of possession as an assured tenancy. *The landlord cannot simply tell a tenant to leave before the end of the agreed term.*

If the tenancy runs on after the end of the fixed term then the landlord can regain possession by giving the required two months notice, as mentioned above.

At the end of the term for which the assured shorthold tenancy has been granted, the landlord has an automatic right to possession. An assured shorthold tenancy will become periodic (will run from week to week) when the initial term of six months has elapsed and the landlord has not brought the tenancy to an end. A periodic tenancy is brought to an end with two months notice.

Assured shorthold tenants, can be evicted only on certain grounds some discretionary, some mandatory (see below). In order for the landlord of an assured shorthold tenant to regain possession of the property, other than issuing a s21 notice, a notice of seeking possession (of property) must be served, giving fourteen days notice of expiry and stating the ground for possession. This notice is similar to a notice to quit, discussed in the previous chapter. Following the fourteen days a court order must be obtained. Although gaining a court order is not complicated, a solicitor will usually be used. Court costs can be awarded against the tenant.

Security of tenure: The ways in which a tenant can lose their home as an assured shorthold tenant

There are a number of circumstances called grounds (mandatory and discretionary) whereby a landlord can start a court action to evict a tenant. The following are the *mandatory* grounds (where the judge must give the landlord possession) and *discretionary* grounds (where the judge does not have to give the landlord possession) on which a court can order possession if the home is subject to an assured tenancy.

The mandatory grounds for possession of a property

There are eight mandatory grounds for possession, which, if proved, leave the court with no choice but to make an order for possession. It is very important that you understand these.

Ground One is used where the landlord has served a notice, no later than at the beginning of the tenancy, warning the tenant that this ground may be used against him/her.

This ground is used where the landlord wishes to recover the property as his or her principal (first and only) home or the spouse's (wife's or husbands) principal home. *The ground is not available to a person who bought the premises for gain (profit) whilst they were occupied.*

Ground Two is available where the property is subject to a mortgage and if the landlord does not pay the mortgage, could lose the home.

Grounds Three and Four relate to holiday lettings.

Ground Five is a special one, applicable to ministers of religion.

Ground Six relates to the demolition or reconstruction of the property.

Ground Seven applies if a tenant dies and in his will leaves the tenancy to someone else: but the landlord must start proceedings against the new tenant within a year of the death if he wants to evict the new tenant.

Ground Eight concerns rent arrears. This ground applies if, both at the date of the serving of the notice seeking possession and at the date of the hearing of the action, the rent is at least 8 weeks in arrears. This is the main ground used by landlords when rent is not being paid. The landlord should understand that in order to get a court order for possession of property for rent arrears then, because of the short-term nature of the Assured shorthold, time is of the essence. If the tenancy is into the third month, it may be easier to wait and serve a two-month notice of termination and get a court order against the occupants separately. One of the advantages of a court order is that you will have details of the tenant's employers and can get an attachment of earnings against the tenant.

The discretionary grounds for possession of a property, which is let on an assured tenancy

As we have seen, the discretionary grounds for possession are those in relation to which the court has some powers over whether or not the landlord can evict. In other words, the final decision is left to the judge. Often the judge will prefer to grant a suspended order first, unless the circumstances are dramatic.

Ground Nine applies when suitable alternative accommodation is available or will be when the possession order takes effect. As we have seen, if the landlord wishes to obtain possession of his or her property in order to use it for other purposes then suitable alternative accommodation has to be provided.

Ground Ten deals with rent arrears as does *ground eleven.* These grounds are distinct from the mandatory grounds, as there does not have to be a fixed arrear in terms of time scale, e.g., 8 weeks. The judge, therefore, has some choice as to whether or not to evict. In practice, this ground will not be relevant to managers of assured shorthold tenancies.

Ground Twelve concerns any broken obligation of the tenancy. As we have seen with the protected tenancy, there are a number of conditions of the tenancy agreement, such as the requirement not to racially or sexually harass a neighbor. Ground Twelve will be used if these conditions are broken.

Ground Thirteen deals with the deterioration of the dwelling as a result of a tenant's neglect. This is connected with the structure of the property and is the same as for a protected tenancy. It puts the responsibility on the tenant to look after the premises.

Ground Fourteen concerns nuisance, annoyance and illegal or immoral use. This is where a tenant or anyone connected with the tenant has caused a nuisance to neighbors.

Ground 14A this ground deals with domestic violence.

Ground 15 concerns the condition of the furniture and tenants neglect. As Ground thirteen puts some responsibility on the tenant to look after the structure of the building so Ground Fifteen makes the tenant responsible for the furniture and fittings.

Ground 16 covers former employees. The premises were let to a former tenant by a landlord seeking possession and the tenant has ceased to be in that employment.

Ground 17 is where a person or that persons agents makes a false or reckless statement and this has caused the landlord to grant the tenancy under false pretences.

The description of the grounds above is intended as a guide only. For a fuller description please refer to the 1988 Housing Act, section 7, Schedule two,) as amended by the 1996 Housing Act) which is available at reference libraries.

****

Ch. 4

Joint Tenancies

Joint tenancies

Tenancy agreements

You have a joint tenancy if you and the other tenants all signed a single tenancy agreement with a landlord when you moved in. If each of you signed a separate agreement with the landlord, you have separate tenancies.

Right to rent

As we discussed, you can only become a private tenant if you have the right to rent. Each joint tenant must have the right to rent. A private landlord or letting agent must carry out a right to rent check before you sign up to a private tenancy.

Paying the rent when you're a joint tenant

Joint tenants are each jointly and individually responsible for paying the rent.

If one tenant moves out without giving notice or doesn't pay their share of the rent, the other joint tenants are responsible for paying it for them. If none of you pay your rent, your landlord can ask any one of you to pay the outstanding rent.

Tenancy deposits

The landlord normally takes a single deposit for the whole of the tenancy. Even if you and the other joint tenants paid separate or different shares to the landlord or agent. If one joint tenant fails to pay their share of the rent or if they cause damage to the property, the landlord is entitled to deduct the shortfall or the costs of the damage from the whole deposit.

You and the other joint tenants decide how to divide up the remaining deposit when it is returned.

Tenancy deposits when a joint tenant moves out

If you are replacing another tenant who is moving out, they may ask you to pay the deposit to them instead. This could cause problems. If the tenant who is moving out has caused any damage to the property or left any unpaid bills, the landlord can deduct these costs from the deposit when you move out. Get advice if you are in this situation. It might be better to ask the landlord to give a new tenancy agreement to you and the other tenants who are staying on.

How you can end a fixed-term joint tenancy

If you have a fixed-term tenancy (for example for 12 months) you can only the tenancy before the fixed term ends if:

- you, the other tenants and your landlord all agree that the tenancy can end early (this is called a 'surrender')
- there is a 'break clause' in your tenancy agreement, which allows you to give notice and end your tenancy early

You need the agreement of the other joint tenants to end your tenancy early.

How to end a joint tenancy that isn't a fixed-term

If you don't have fixed-term tenancy or it has ended and not been renewed, you or any other joint tenant can end the tenancy by giving a valid notice to quit to the landlord. You can do this with or without the agreement of the other joint tenants. The tenancy ends for all the joint tenants. When the notice to quit expires none of you has the right to continue living there.

Leaving a joint tenancy

If you want to leave a joint tenancy and the others want to stay it is usually best to discuss it with the other joint tenants before you take any action.

If they don't want to move out, they can try to negotiate a new agreement with the landlord. The remaining tenants may be able to find another person to become a joint tenant with them. They must get the landlord's agreement for this. Or the remaining tenants could all agree to stay on and pay the rent between them.

However if the joint tenancy has not been ended the landlord could still ask you to pay any arrears if the rent is not fully paid, even if you are no longer living there.

Eviction of joint tenants

Your landlord cannot evict one joint tenant without evicting all the others.

Your landlord may be able to end the tenancy and offer a new one to the remaining tenants. Talk to your landlord as soon as possible if you are in this situation and you want to stay.

.

Relationship breakdown

Your landlord could grant you a new tenancy in your name only if the joint tenancy with your ex-partner has been properly ended. You may also have other rights. For example:

- it may be possible for court to transfer the tenancy into your name – even if the other joint tenant won't agree to it
- it may be possible to stop the other joint tenant from ending the tenancy by applying for an occupation order or an injunction
- if you have experienced domestic violence, it may be possible to take legal action such as an injunction

.

Problems with other joint tenants

If you have a problem with another joint tenant you probably have to sort this out yourself. Landlords are usually reluctant to get involved, although council or housing associations are more likely to get involved than private landlords.

****

Ch. 5

Rent and Other Charges

_____

The payment of rent and other financial matters
If a tenancy is protected under the Rent Act 1977, as described earlier there is the right to apply to the Rent Officer for the setting of a fair rent for the property. However, as described earlier, the incidence of Rent Act Protected Tenancies has diminished to almost zero.

The assured tenant
The assured tenant has far fewer rights in relation to rent control than the protected tenant. The Housing Act 1988 allows a landlord to charge whatever he likes. There is no right to a fair or reasonable rent with an assured tenancy. If the tenancy is assured then there will usually be a formula in the tenancy which will provide guidance for rent increases. If not then the landlord can set what rent he or she likes within reason. If the amount is unreasonable then the tenant can refer the matter to the local Rent Assessment Committee. The rent can sometimes be negotiated at the outset of the tenancy. This rent has to be paid as long as the contractual term of the tenancy lasts. Once the contractual term has expired, the landlord is entitled to continue to charge the same rent.

On expiry of an assured shorthold the landlord is free to grant a new tenancy and set the rent to a level that is compatible with the market.

Details of the local Rent Assessment Committee can be obtained from the Rent Officer Service at your local authority.

Local housing allowance (LHA) (housing benefit) for people who rent a home from a private landlord.

Local housing allowance is housing benefit for private sector tenants It's usually paid directly to you and you pay your landlord. Local housing allowance is housing benefit that helps pay the rent and some service charges (if applicable) if you rent from a private landlord. It's a benefit administered by your local council. LHA has many of the same rules as housing benefit, but there are some extra rules that limit the amount of help you can get for a private rented home. LHA is usually paid direct to you rather than to your landlord.

Claim LHA

You can claim local housing allowance if you are a private tenant who needs help with paying the rent. You may be entitled to this housing benefit if you are working or if you claim benefits. Local Housing Allowance (LHA) is used to work out Housing Benefit for tenants who rent privately. How much you get is usually based on:

- where you live
- your household size
- your income - including benefits, pensions and savings (over £6,000)
- your circumstances

Your LHA claim is routinely reassessed after 12 months. Your claim may be reassessed at any time if your circumstances change.

How LHA is calculated

The amount of LHA you can get depends on your income and savings and if any non-dependants live with you, for example adult children.

The amount of LHA you receive also depends on the maximum rent allowed for properties in your area and the number of rooms the council decides you need.

You can rent a home of any size or price, but your housing benefit claim is limited. You have to make up any rent shortfall.

Maximum LHA amounts

There are limits on the amount of LHA you can get. The maximum weekly LHA rate limits (2017-2018) are:

£260.64 for a room in shared accommodation
£260.64 for 1 bedroom accommodation
£302.33 for 2 bedroom accommodation
£354.46 for 3 bedroom accommodation
£417.02 for 4 bedroom accommodation

The amount of LHA you are eligible for depends on where you live. Local limits are based on the cheapest 30% of properties in an area.

Rooms allowed when calculating LHA

You are assessed as needing a bedroom for the following people in your home:

- an adult couple
- another person aged 16 or over
- any two children of the same sex up to the age of 16
- any two children regardless of sex under the age of 10

any other child

An extra bedroom can be allowed if you:
- have a foster child or children
- have a severely disabled child who needs their own room
- or your partner are disabled and a carer provides regular overnight care
- have a child who is away on duty with the armed forces and intends to return home
- You cannot be allowed more than four bedrooms for the purposes of calculating your LHA.

If you're aged under 35

You are usually only entitled to LHA at the reduced shared accommodation rate if you are a single person under age 35 without children or you live in shared accommodation.

How often is housing benefit paid?

Payment of housing benefit depends on how often you pay rent. Housing benefit is not paid in advance. Each payment covers a past period.

Private landlords usually expect rent to be paid in advance, so you need to budget for this.

When LHA can be paid direct to landlords

Your council must make your LHA payments direct to your landlord if:

- you have rent arrears of eight weeks or more
- deductions are being made from your benefits for rent arrears
- In some cases, the council can choose to pay your LHA direct to your landlord. They could do this if you have failed to pay the rent in the past or you have problems paying your rent because of a medical condition. The council can pay LHA direct to your landlord if this will help you keep your tenancy.

If you have support needs, the council can pay LHA to your landlord to encourage them to keep you as a tenant. The council will consult you and people supporting you before deciding to pay LHA direct to your landlord. This may include your doctor, support worker, probation officer and others who know about your situation.

Council Tax Support

If you are in receipt of benefits you may get help with your council tax through Council tax Support. Your local authority will advise you on this.

****

Ch. 6

The Right to Quiet Enjoyment of a Home

Earlier, we saw that when a tenancy agreement is signed, the landlord is contracting to give quiet enjoyment of the tenants home. This means that they have the right to live peacefully in the home without harassment.

The landlord is obliged not to do anything that will disturb the right to the quiet enjoyment of the home. The most serious breach of this right would be for the landlord to wrongfully evict a tenant.

Eviction: what can be done against unlawful eviction

It is a criminal offence for a landlord unlawfully to evict a residential occupier (whether or not a tenant!). The occupier has protection under the Protection from Eviction Act 1977 section 1(2). If the tenant or occupier is unlawfully evicted his/her first course should be to seek an injunction compelling the landlord to readmit him/her to the premises. It is an unfortunate fact but many landlords will attempt to evict tenants forcefully. In doing so they break the law.

The Deregulation Act 2015 has introduced a new provision which deals with 'retaliatory evictions'. This is where the landlord has decided to issue a s21 notice on the tenant because they have complained about the landlords service (for example repairs to the property) or unreasonable behaviour. If it can be proven that the notice was a 'retaliatory notice' then this will be invalid.

However, the landlord may, on termination of the tenancy, recover possession without a court order if the agreement was entered into after 15th January 1989 and it falls into one of the following six situations:

- The occupier shares any accommodation with the landlord and the landlord occupies the premises as his or her only or principal home.
- The occupier shares any of the accommodation with a member of the landlords family, that person occupies the premises as their only or principal home, and the landlord occupies as his or her only or principal home premises in the same building.
- The tenancy or license was granted temporarily to an occupier who entered the premises as a trespasser.
- The tenancy or license gives the right to occupy for the purposes of a holiday.
- The tenancy or license is rent-free.
- The license relates to occupation of a hostel.

There is also a section in the 1977 Protection from Eviction Act which provides a defense for otherwise unlawful eviction and that is that the landlord may repossess if it is thought that the tenant no longer lives on the premises. It is important to note that, in order for such action to be seen as a crime under the 1977 Protection from Eviction Act, the intention of the landlord to evict must be proved.

However, there is another offence, namely harassment, which also needs to be proved. Even if the landlord is not guilty of permanently depriving a tenant of their home he/she could be guilty of harassment. Such actions as cutting off services, deliberately allowing the premises to fall into a state of disrepair, or even forcing unwanted sexual attentions, all constitute harassment and a breach of the right to *quiet enjoyment*.

The 1977 Protection from Eviction Act also prohibits the use of violence to gain entry to premises. Even in situations where the landlord has the right to gain entry without a court order it is an offence to use violence.

What can be done against unlawful evictions?

There are two main remedies for unlawful eviction: damages and, as stated above, an injunction.

The injunction

An injunction is an order from the court requiring a person to do, or not to do something. In the case of eviction the court can grant an injunction requiring the landlord to allow a tenant back into occupation of the premises. In the case of harassment an order can be made preventing the landlord from harassing the tenant. Failure to comply with an injunction is contempt of court and can result in a fine or imprisonment.

Damages

In some cases the tenant can press for *financial compensation* following unlawful eviction. Financial compensation may have to be paid in cases where financial loss has occurred or in cases where personal hardship alone has occurred. The tenant can also press for *special damages,* which means that the tenant may recover the definable out-of-pocket expenses. These could be expenses arising as a result of having to stay in a hotel because of the eviction. Receipts must be kept in that case. There are also *general damages,* which can be awarded in compensation for stress, suffering and inconvenience.

A tenant may also seek *exemplary damages* where it can be proved that the landlord has disregarded the law deliberately with the intention of making a profit out of the displacement of the tenant.

****

Ch. 7

Repairs-Landlords/Tenants Obligations

Repairs and improvements generally: The landlord and tenants obligations

Repairs are essential works to keep the property in good order. Improvements and alterations to the property, e.g. the installation of a shower.

As we have seen, most tenancies are periodic, i.e. week-to-week or month-to-month. If a tenancy falls into this category, or is a fixed-term tenancy for less than seven years, and began after October 1961, then a landlord is legally responsible for most major repairs to the flat or house.

If a tenancy began after 15th January 1989 then, in addition to the above responsibility, the landlord is also responsible for repairs to common parts and service fittings.

The area of law dealing with the landlord and tenants repairing obligations is the 1985 Landlord and Tenant Act, section 11. This section of the Act is known as a covenant and cannot be excluded by informal agreement between landlord and tenant. In other words the landlord is legally responsible whether he or she likes it or not.

Parties to a tenancy, however, may make an application to a court mutually to vary or exclude this section.

Example of repairs a landlord is responsible for:

- Leaking roofs and guttering.
- Rotting windows.
- Rising damp.
- Damp walls.
- Faulty electrical wiring.
- Dangerous ceilings and staircases.
- Faulty gas and water pipes.
- Broken water heaters and boilers.
- Broken lavatories, sinks or baths.

In shared housing the landlord must see that shared halls, stairways, kitchens and bathrooms are maintained and kept clean and lit.

Normally, tenants are responsible only for minor repairs, e.g., broken door handles, cupboard doors, etc. Tenants will also be responsible for decorations unless they have been damaged as a result of the landlord's failure to do repair.

A landlord will be responsible for repairs only if the repair has been reported. It is therefore important to report repairs in writing and keep a copy. If the repair is not carried out then action can be taken. Damages can also be claimed.

Compensation can be claimed, with the appropriate amount being the reduction in the value of the premises to the tenant caused by the landlord's failure to repair. If the tenant carries out the repairs then the amount expended will represent the decrease in value.

The tenant does not have the right to withhold rent because of a breach of repairing covenant by the landlord. However, depending on the repair, the landlord will not have a very strong case in court if rent is withheld.

Reporting repairs to landlords

The tenant has to tell the landlord or the person collecting the rent straight away when a repair needs doing. It is advisable that it is in writing, listing the repairs that need to be done.

Once a tenant has reported a repair the landlord must do it within a reasonable period of time. What is reasonable will depend on the nature of the repair. If certain emergency work needs to be done by the council, such as leaking guttering or drains a notice can be served ordering the landlord to do the work within a short time. In exceptional cases if a home cannot be made habitable at reasonable cost the council may declare that the house must no longer be used, in which case the council has a legal duty to re-house a tenant.

If after the council has served notice the landlord still does not do the work, the council can send in its own builder or, in some cases take the landlord to court. A tenant must allow a landlord access to do repairs. The landlord has to give twenty-four hours notice of wishing to gain access.

The tenants rights whilst repairs are being carried out

The landlord must ensure that the repairs are done in an orderly and efficient way with minimum inconvenience to the tenant. If the works are disruptive or if property or decorations are damaged the tenant can apply to the court for compensation or, if necessary, for an order to make the landlord behave reasonably.

If the landlord genuinely needs the house empty to do the work he/she can ask the tenant to vacate it and can if necessary get a court order against the tenant. A written agreement should be drawn up making it clear that the tenant can move back in when the repairs are completed and stating what the arrangements for fuel charges and rent are. If a person is an assured tenant the landlord could get a court order to make that person give up the home permanently if there is work to be done with him/her in occupation.

Can the landlord put the rent up after doing repairs?

If there is a service charge for maintenance, the landlord may be able to pass on the cost of the work(s).

Tenants rights to make improvements to a property

Unlike carrying out repairs the tenant will not normally have the right to insist that the landlord make actual alterations to the home. However, a tenant needs the following amenities and the law states that you should have:

- Bath or shower.
- Wash hand basin.
- Hot and cold water at each bath, basin or shower.
- An indoor toilet.

If these amenities do not exist then the tenant can contact the council's Environmental Health Officer. An improvement notice can be served on the landlord ordering him to put the amenity in.

Disabled tenants

If a tenant is disabled he/she may need special items of equipment in the accommodation. The local authority may help in providing and, occasionally, paying for these. The tenant will need to obtain the permission of the landlord. If you require more information then contact the social services department locally.

The Equality Act 2010

The Equality Act 2010 has introduced a new duty on landlords (from October 2010) to consent to changes in common parts of residential or mixed-use buildings in England, Wales and Scotland. This means that if a disabled tenant or occupier who uses or intends to use premises in a building as his or her main home requests physical changes to common parts to reduce or avoid a disadvantage suffered in comparison with non-disabled people, the landlord must within a reasonable time consult all other likely to be affected by the changes and, having considered the views of those consulted, take whatever steps are reasonable to avoid the disadvantage. If changes to the common parts are considered reasonable the landlord must first enter into a written agreement that the disabled person organizes and pays for the work and for restoration of the common parts when the disabled person leaves the property.

The agreement will bind the landlord's successors but not the disabled person's successors. So the landlord may wish to insist that the works are reinstated before the disabled person leaves.

Shared housing. The position of tenants in shared houses (Houses in Multiple Occupation)

A major change to improve standards of shared housing was introduced in 2006. The parts of the Housing Act 2004 relating to the licensing of HMO's (Houses in Multiple Occupation) and the new Health and Safety Rating System for assessing property conditions came into effect on 6rh April 2006. The Act requires landlords of many HMO's to apply for licences. The HMO's that need to be licensed are those with:

- Three or more storeys, which are
- Occupied by five or more people forming two or more households (i.e. people not related, living together as a couple etc) and
- Which have an element of shared facilities (eg kitchen, bathroom etc)

As far as licensing is concerned, attics and basements are included as storeys if they are used as living accommodation. Previously, HMO's were only defined as houses converted into flats or bedsits, but the new Act widens this definition and many more types of shared houses are now included.

A local authority will have a list of designated properties will have a list of those properties which are designated HMO's and they will need to be licensed.

Usually, landlords will need to apply to a local authority private sector unit for licences. It has been illegal for landlords to manage designated properties without a licence since July 2006.

Landlords will have to complete an application form and pay a fee, the local authority will then assess whether the property is suitable for the number of people the landlord wants to rent it to. In most case, the local authority, their agents, will visit a property to assess facilities and also fire precautions. A decision will then be taken to grant a license. There is a fee for registration, councils set the fee and the ones shown below are indicative of a southern local authority:

Shared houses-five sharers landlords first house £640
Subsequent house £590
Plus £10 each additional occupier over five

Hostels
10 occupiers £690
20 occupiers £790
50 occupiers £1100
75 occupiers £1340

In summary, The landlord of a HMO has certain duties under the regulations to his tenants:

Duty to provide information
The manager (this means that whoever is charged with the management of the building) must ensure that:

- His name, address and telephone number are available to each household in the HMO
- These details are also clearly displayed in a prominent position in the HMO.

The manager should maintain a log book to record all events at the property such as:

- Testing of fire alarms
- Testing of fire fighting equipment
- Gas safety certificate
- Electrical report
- Inspection and wants of repair

Duty to take safety measures

The manager must ensure that all means of escape from fire in the property are kept free from obstruction and in good order as should all fire alarms and equipment. The manager should ensure that the structure is designed and maintained in a safe condition, and also take steps to protect occupiers from injury. In properties with four or more occupants, the Regulations provide that fire escape notices be clearly displayed.

Duty to maintain water supply drainage

The manager must ensure that the water supply and drainage system serving the property are maintained in a good working condition. More specifically, water fittings should be protected from frost and all water storage tanks should be provided with covers.

Duty to supply and maintain gas and electricity

The manager must supply the local housing authority within 7 days of receiving a written request a safety certificate. The manager must ensure that the fixed electrical installation is checked at least once every three years by a suitably qualified electrician and supply this to the LHA on written request. In addition to the above, there is a duty to maintain common parts, fixtures, fittings and appliances. There is a duty to maintain living accommodation and to provide waste disposal facilities.

Powers of the local authority in relation to HMO's

It is essential to ensure that, if you have invested in a HMO that you manage it rigorously because local authorities have sweeping powers to fine landlords and to revoke licenses. A local authority can prosecute a landlord who does not obtain a license for a HMO.

Safety generally for all landlords-the regulations

The main product safety regulations relevant to the lettings industry are:

Gas safety

The Gas safety (Installation and use) Regulations 1998
The Gas Cooking Appliances (safety) Regulations 1989
Heating Appliances(Fireguard) (safety) Regulations 1991
Gas Appliances(Safety) Regulations 1995

All of the above are based on the fact that the supply of gas and the appliances in a dwelling are safe. A Gas Safety certificate is required to validate this.

Furniture Safety

Furniture and Furnishings (Fire) (Safety) Regulations 1988 and 1993 (as amended). Landlords and lettings agents are included in these regulations. The regulations set high standards for fire resistance for domestic upholstered furniture and other products containing upholstery.

The main provisions are:

- Upholstered articles (i.e. beds, sofas, armchairs etc) must have fire resistant filling material.
- Upholstered articles must have passed a match resistant test or, if of certain kinds (such as cotton or silk) be used with a fire resistant interliner.
- The combination of the cover fabric and the filling material must have passed a cigarette resistance test.

The landlord should inspect property for non-compliant items before letting and replace with compliant items.

Electrical Safety

Electrical Equipment (Safety) Regulations 1994

Plugs and Sockets etc. (Safety) Regulations 1994.

The Electrical Equipment Regulations came into force in January 1995. Both sets of regulations relate to the supply of electrical equipment designed with a working voltage of between 50 and 1000 volts a.c. (or between 75 and 1000 volts d.c.) the regulations cover all the mains voltage household electrical goods including cookers, kettles, toasters, electric blankets, washing machines, immersion heaters etc. The regulations do not apply to items attached to land. This is generally considered to exclude the fixed wiring and built in appliances (e.g. central heating systems) from the regulations.

The availability of grants
Disabled Facilities Grant
The only mandatory grant is the Disabled Facilities Grant, given to those in need, which has been assessed by an Occupational Therapist-the grant has a ceiling. Information of which can be obtained from the local authority. As the name suggests it is for those who are disabled and are n need of works which will make the property accessible and usable for disabled people. For information about other grants available contact the local authority dealing with your area.

New regulations on Smoke and Carbon Monoxide detectors
From October 2015, all landlords, regardless of whether public or private sector, will be required to install working smoke and carbon monoxide alarms in their properties, on each floor. The carbon monoxide alarms will need to be placed in high risk areas, i.e., where there are gas appliances such as boilers or fires. Carbon monoxide detectors will not be required in properties where there are no gas or solid fuel appliances. A civil penalty of up to £5,000 will apply to landlords who fail to comply with this legislation.

Sanitation health and hygiene
Local authorities have a duty to serve an owner with a notice requiring the provision of a WC when a property has insufficient

sanitation, sanitation meaning toilet waste disposal. They will also serve notice if it is thought that the existing sanitation is inadequate and is harmful to health or is a nuisance.

Local authorities have similar powers under various Public Health Acts to require owners to put right bad drains and sewers, also food storage facilities and vermin, plus the containing of disease. The Environmental Health Department, if it considers the problem bad enough will serve a notice requiring the landlord to put the defect right. In certain cases the local authority can actually do the work and require the landlord to pay for it. This is called work in default.

****

Ch. 8

What Should Be Provided Under the Tenancy

Furniture

A landlords decision whether or not to furnish property will depend on the sort of tenant that he is aiming to find. The actual legal distinction between a furnished property and an unfurnished property has faded into insignificance.

If a landlord does let a property as furnished then the following would be the absolute minimum:

- Seating, such as sofa and armchair

- Cabinet or sideboard

- Kitchen tables and chairs

- Cooker and refrigerator

- Bedroom furniture

Even unfurnished lets, however, are expected to come complete with a basic standard of furniture, particularly carpets and kitchen goods. If the landlord does supply electrical equipment then he or she is able to disclaim any repairing responsibility for it, but this must be mentioned in the tenancy agreement.

Insurance

Strictly speaking, there is no duty on either landlord or tenant to insure the property. However, it is highly advisable for the landlord to provide buildings insurance as he/she stands to lose a lot more in the event of fire or other disaster than the tenant. A landlord letting property for a first time would be well advised to consult his/ her insurance company before letting as there are different criteria to observe when a property is let and not to inform the company could invalidate the policy.

At the end of the tenancy

The tenancy agreement will normally spell out the obligations of the tenant at the end of the term. Essentially, the tenant will have an obligation to:

* have kept the interior clean and tidy and in a good state of repair and decoration
* have not caused any damage
* have replaced anything that they have broken
* replace or pay for the repair of anything that they have damaged
* pay for the laundering of the linen
* pay for any other laundering
* put anything that they have moved or removed back to how it was

Sometimes a tenancy agreement will include for the tenants paying for anything that is soiled at their own expense, although sensible wear and tear is allowed for.

The landlord will normally be able to recover any loss from the deposit that the tenant has given on entering the premises. However, sometimes, the tenants will withhold rent for the last month in order to recoup their deposit. This has become more difficult since the introduction of the tenancy deposit schemes, described earlier. It is up to the landlord to negotiate re-imbursement for any damage caused, but this should be within reason. There is a remedy, which can be pursued in the Small Claims court if the tenants refuse to pay but this is rarely successful.

****

Ch. 9

Regaining Possession of a Property

....

Fast-track possession

Previously, a landlord will have served a section 21 notice on the tenant at the start of the tenancy. However, following the passage of the Deregulation Act 2015, the landlord can no longer do this and must serve the notice after the tenant has been in occupation for four months. This brings the tenancy to an end on the day of expiry, i.e. on the day of expiry of the six month period, or 12 month period, whichever is appropriate. It should be noted that if a landlord takes a deposit from the tenant then every deposit must be registered with the appropriate deposit service before the landlord can serve the s21 notice.

It should also be noted that if a section 21 notice is served after the end of the fixed term giving two months notice then the notice should be a section 21 (b). This is important as a service of the incorrect notice can delay proceedings. For all AST's issued after October 1st 2015, a Form 6a is served (se appendix).

On expiry of the notice, if it is the landlord's intention to take possession of the property then the tenants should leave. It is worthwhile writing a letter to the tenants one month before expiry reminding them that they should leave.

In the event of the tenant refusing to leave, then the landlord has to then follow a process termed 'fast track possession'. This entails filling in the appropriate forms (N5B) which can be accessed from:

www.gov.uk/accelerated-possession-eviction. the process is online and costs £355 (2017/2018)

Assuming that a valid section 21 notice has been served on the tenant, the accelerated possession proceedings can begin and the forms completed online which are then lodged with the court dealing with the area where the property is situated. In order to grant the accelerated possession order the court will require the following:

The assured shorthold agreement
The section 21 notice (or form 6a)
Evidence of service of the section 21 notice

The best form of service of the s21 notice is by hand. If the notice has already served then evidence that the tenant has received it will be required.

A copy must also be served on the tenant. This will be done by the court although it might help if the landlord also serves a copy informing the tenant that they are taking proceedings. If the tenant disputes the possession proceedings in any way they will have 14 days to reply to the court. If the case is well founded and the paperwork is in order then there should be no case for defence. Once the accelerated possession order has been granted then this will need to be served on the tenant, giving them 14 days to vacate. In certain circumstances, if the tenant pleads hardship the court can grant extra time to leave, six weeks as opposed to two weeks. If they still do not vacate then an application will need to be made to court for a bailiffs warrant to evict the tenants.

An accelerated possession order remains in force for six years from the date it was granted.

Going to court to end the tenancy

There may come a time when the landlord needs to go to court to regain possession of a property. This will usually arise when the contract has been breached by the tenant, for non-payment of rent or for some other breach such as nuisance or harassment. As we have seen, a tenancy can be brought to an end in a court on one of the grounds for possession. However, as the tenancy will usually be an assured shorthold then it is necessary to consider whether the landlord is in a position to give two months notice and withhold the deposit, as opposed to going to court. The act of withholding the deposit will entail the landlord refusing to authorize the payment to the tenant online. This then brings arbitration into the frame. Deposit schemes have an arbitration system as an integral part of the scheme.

If the landlord decides, for whatever reason, to go to court, then any move to regain the property for breach of agreement will commence in the county court in the area in which the property is. The first steps in ending the tenancy will necessitate the serving of a notice of seeking possession using one of the Grounds for Possession detailed earlier in the book. If the tenancy is protected then 28 days must be given, the notice must be in prescribed form and served on the tenant personally (preferably).

If the tenancy is an assured shorthold, which is more often the case now, then 14 days notice of seeking possession can be used. In all cases the ground to be relied upon must be clearly outlined in the notice. If the case is more complex, then this will entail a particulars of claim being prepared, usually by a solicitor, as opposed to a standard possession form.

A fee is paid when sending the particulars to court, which should be checked with the local county court. The standard form which the landlord uses for routine rent arrears cases is called the N119 and the accompanying summons is called the N5. Both of these forms can be obtained from the court or from :

justice.gov.uk/HMCTS/FormFinder.do When completed, the forms should be sent in duplicate to the county court and a copy retained for the landlord.

The court will send a copy of the particulars of claim and the summons to the tenant. They will send the landlord a form which gives him a case number and court date to appear, known as the return date.

On the return date, the landlord will arrive at court at least 15 minutes early. He can represent yourself in simple cases but will be advised to use a solicitor for more contentious cases.

If the tenant is present then they will have a chance to defend themselves.

A number of orders are available. However, if a landlord has gone to court on the mandatory ground eight then if the fact is proved then they will get possession immediately. If not, then the judge can grant an order, suspended whilst the tenant finds time to pay.

In a lot of cases, it is more expedient for a landlord to serve notice-requiring possession, if the tenancy has reached the end of the period, and then wait two months before the property is regained. This saves the cost and time of going to court particularly if the ground is one of nuisance or other, which will involve solicitors.

If the landlord regains possession of your property midway through the contractual term then he will have to complete the possession process by use of bailiff, pay a fee and fill in another form, Warrant for Possession of Land.

****

Ch. 10

Public Sector Tenancies

Renting from a social housing landlord
Who is a tenant of a social housing landlord?
You are a tenant of a social housing landlord if you are a tenant of:

a local authority. These are district councils and London borough councils; or
a housing association; or
a housing co-operative.

Local authority tenants
If you are a tenant of a local authority you are likely to be a secure tenant or an introductory tenant. In England, from 1 April 2012, local authorities can also grant flexible tenancies.

Housing association and housing co-operative tenants
Tenancy began before 15 January 1989
If you are a housing association or housing co-operative tenant and your tenancy began before 15 January 1989, you will be a secure tenant. For details about the rights a secure tenant has, see below.

Tenancy began on or after 15 January 1989
If you are a housing association or housing co-operative tenant and your tenancy began on or after 15 January 1989, you are likely to be

an assured tenant. Some association tenants may be starter tenants for the first 12 to 18 months. A starter tenancy is a type of assured shorthold tenancy. In England, from 1 April 2012, housing associations can use assured shorthold tenancies for tenancies other than starter tenancies.

Rights of secure tenants

As a secure tenant you have the right to stay in the accommodation unless your landlord can convince the court that there are special reasons to evict you, for example, you have rent arrears, damaged property or broken some other term of the agreement. As well as the right to stay in your home as long as you keep to the terms of the tenancy, you will also have other rights by law.

These include the right:

- to have certain repairs carried out by your landlord
- to carry out certain repairs and to do improvements yourself - see under heading Repairs and improvements
- to sublet part of your home with your landlord's permission
- to take in lodgers without your landlord's permission
- to exchange your home with certain other social housing tenants
- if you are a local authority tenant, the right to vote to transfer to another landlord
- to be kept informed about things relating to your tenancy
- to buy your home.

- if you are a housing association tenant whose tenancy started before 15 January 1989, the right to a 'fair rent' - see under heading Fixing and increasing the rent
- for your spouse, civil partner, other partner or in some cases a resident member of your family, to take over the tenancy on your death (the right of 'succession')
- to assign (pass on) the tenancy to a person who has the right of 'succession' to the tenancy. This is sometimes difficult to enforce
- if you are a local authority tenant, to take over the management of the estate with other tenants by setting up a Tenant Management Organisation
- not to be discriminated against because of your disability, gender reassignment, pregnancy and maternity, race, religion or belief, sex or sexual orientation.

You will usually have a written tenancy agreement which may give you more rights than those set out above.

Complaints about secure tenancies

Each social housing landlord must have a clear policy and procedure on dealing with complaints. You should have the opportunity to complain in a range of ways. If after using your landlord's complaints procedure you are still dissatisfied, you can complain to an Ombudsman about certain problems. In England, if you are a local authority tenant this will be the Local Government Ombudsman, and if you are a housing association tenant it will be the Housing Ombudsman. If you have suffered discrimination, you can complain about this to the Ombudsman. In Wales, you can complain to the Public Services Ombudsman for Wales.

Rights of assured tenants

As an assured tenant you have the right to stay in your accommodation unless your landlord can convince the court there are reasons to evict you, for example, that there are rent arrears, damage to the property, or that another of the terms of the agreement has been broken.

As an assured tenant you can enforce your rights, for example, to get repairs done, without worrying about getting evicted. As well as the right to stay in your home as long as you keep to the terms of the tenancy you will also have other rights by law including:-

- the right to have the accommodation kept in a reasonable state of repair
- the right to carry out minor repairs yourself and to receive payment for these from your landlord - see under heading Repairs and improvements
- the right for your spouse, civil partner or other partner to take over the tenancy on your death (the right of 'succession')
- the right not to be treated unfairly by your landlord because of your disability, gender reassignment, pregnancy and maternity, race, religion or belief, sex or sexuality.

You will usually have a written tenancy agreement which may give you more rights than those set out above.

Complaints about assured tenancies

Each housing association must have a clear policy and procedure on dealing with complaints. You should have the opportunity to complain in a range of ways. If after using your landlord's complaints procedure you are still dissatisfied, you can complain in England, to the Housing Ombudsman, or in Wales, to the Public Services Ombudsman for Wales.

Starter tenancies and assured shorthold tenancies

A starter tenancy is the name often used by housing associations to describe an assured shorthold tenancy. Starter tenancies are probationary tenancies which allow a landlord to evict you more easily if you break the terms of your tenancy agreement.

A starter tenancy generally lasts for 12 months, although they can be extended to 18 months. As long as no action has been taken by the landlord to end the tenancy within the starter period, the starter tenant can then become an assured or longer-term assured shorthold tenant in England, or an assured tenant in Wales.

In England, housing associations can use assured shorthold tenancies for tenancies other than starter tenancies. They are likely to last for a fixed term of five years or more, but in some cases will last for two years. These tenancies may also be on 'affordable rent' terms.

In England, if you have an assured shorthold tenancy of a fixed term of two years or more with a housing association landlord, you will generally have similar rights to an assured tenant. However, if you have a fixed term tenancy, you only have the right to stay in your home for the length of the fixed term.

Complaints about starter and assured shorthold tenancies

Each housing association must have a clear policy and procedure on dealing with complaints. You should have the opportunity to complain in a range of ways. If after using your landlord's complaints procedure you are still dissatisfied, you can complain in England, to the Housing Ombudsman, or in Wales, to the Public Services Ombudsman for Wales.

Fixing and increasing the rent-Secure tenants
Local authority tenancies

Rents for local authority tenants are fixed according to the local authority's housing policy and the amount of money they get from central government. You cannot control the amount of rent payable, but may be able to claim housing benefit to help pay it.

Housing association and housing co-operative tenancies which began before 15 January 1989

If you are a housing association or housing co-operative tenant whose tenancy started before 15 January 1989 you are a secure tenant, but your rent is generally a 'fair rent' registered by the Rent Officer. The housing association or co-operative will usually have had the rent registered.

Once a rent has been registered, a new rent cannot usually be considered for the accommodation for two years. The rent can only be increased if:-

- you ask for a new fair rent assessment after two years
- your landlord asks for a new fair rent assessment after one year and nine months, although any new rent would not become effective until the end of two years.

An application for a rent increase can be made earlier, but only if the tenancy has changed drastically or if you and your landlord apply together. If you need help paying the rent you may be able to claim housing benefit.

Assured tenants-Housing association or housing co-operative tenancies which began on or after 15 January 1989

Many housing association tenants whose tenancy started on or after 15 January 1989 are assured tenants. If you are an assured tenant, your rent is the rent you agreed to pay your landlord at the beginning of the tenancy and should be covered in your tenancy agreement. The tenancy agreement should also state when and how the rent can be increased.

In England, most housing associations and housing co-operatives are registered with the Homes and Communities Agency and must follow standards and procedures set down by this regulatory body. They are sometimes known as social landlords. They set rents in accordance with government guidance and tenants have to be given clear information about how their rent and service charges are set and how they can be changed.

You may have the right to apply to a Rent Assessment Committee if you do not agree to a rent increase.

In Wales, housing associations must manage their housing to standards set by the Welsh Government. You must be informed in writing, and in advance about any changes in your rent. You should be given at least 28 days notice of any increase. You may have the right to apply to a Rent Assessment Committee if you do not agree to a rent increase.

If you are a housing association tenant in Wales, there is a leaflet explaining your rights called The Guarantee for Housing Association Residents. You can find this on the Welsh Government website at: www.new.wales.gov.uk.

If you want to apply to a Rent Assessment Committee you should consult an experienced adviser, for example, a Citizens Advice Bureau. If you need help paying the rent you may be able to claim housing benefit. You may also be entitled to other benefits if you are on a low income or you are unemployed.

To work out which other benefits you may be entitled to, you should consult an experienced adviser, for example, a Citizens Advice Bureau.

Affordable rent
Affordable rent is a type of social housing provided in England by social housing landlords.

The rent is called 'affordable' but it is a higher rent than would normally be charged for social housing. The landlord can charge up to 80% of what it would cost if you were renting the property privately. The extra money from affordable rent homes goes towards building more new social housing.

In most cases, tenancies on affordable rent terms are granted by housing associations. Where the landlord is a housing association, the type of tenancy granted is either an assured or an assured shorthold tenancy. In some cases, a local authority may grant a tenancy on affordable rent terms. Where it does, the tenancy type is either a secure or a flexible tenancy.

An affordable rent can be increased once a year. The maximum amount that an affordable rent can be increased by is Retail Price Index (RPI) + 0.5 %.

If you are on benefits or have a low income you may qualify for housing benefit to help pay some or all of the affordable rent.

Repairs and improvements
As a tenant you have the right to have your accommodation kept in a reasonable state of repair. You have also an obligation to look after the accommodation. The tenancy agreement may give more details of both your landlord's and your responsibilities in carrying out repairs and you should check this. We have discussed repairs earlier in the book.

Certain repairs will almost always be your landlord's responsibility, whether or not they are specifically mentioned in the tenancy agreement. These are:-

- the structure and exterior of the premises (such as walls, floors and window frames), and the drains, gutters and external pipes. If the property is a house, the essential means of access to it, such as steps from the street, are also included in 'structure and exterior'. It also includes garden paths and steps
- the water and gas pipes and electrical wiring (including, for example, taps and sockets)
- the basins, sinks, baths and toilets
- fixed heaters (for example, gas fires) and water heaters but not gas or electric cookers.

The Right to repair

Tenants of local authorities and other social landlords (including housing associations) can use 'right to repair' schemes to claim compensation for repairs which the landlord does not carry out within a set timescale.

Under the scheme, if repairs are not carried out within a fixed time scale, you can notify your landlord that you want a different contractor to do the job. The local authority must appoint a new contractor and set another time limit. You can then claim compensation if the repair is not carried out within the new time limit.

As a local authority tenant, you can currently use the 'right to repair' scheme for repairs which your landlord estimates would cost up to £250. You can also claim up to £50 compensation. Twenty types of repairs qualify for the scheme, including insecure doors, broken entry phone systems, blocked sinks and leaking roofs.

A repair will not qualify for the scheme if the local authority has fewer than 100 properties, is not responsible for the repair or if the authority decides it would cost more than £250.

If you're the tenant of another social landlord, such as a housing association, you are entitled to compensation if you report a repair or maintenance problem which affects your health, safety or security and your landlord fails twice to make the repair within the set timescale.

There is a flat rate award which is currently £10, plus £2 a day up to a total of £50, for each day the repair remains outstanding. A maximum cost for an eligible repair may be set by the individual landlord.

Improvements

As a local authority tenant if you make certain improvements to your home, for example, loft insulation, draught proofing, new baths, basins and toilets and security measures, you can apply for compensation for doing so when you move out. You will not be eligible for this compensation if you buy your home.

Disabled tenants

If you are disabled, you may be able to have alterations carried out to your home. You may first have to get the need for any alterations assessed by the social services department. Alterations could include the installation of a stair lift or hoist or adaptation of a bathroom or toilet. If you want to get an alteration carried out you should consult an experienced adviser, for example, at a Citizens Advice Bureau. A disabled tenant may also be able to get a disabled facilities grant to make the home more suitable.

Gas appliances

Your landlord must make sure that any gas appliances in residential premises are safe. They must arrange for safety checks on appliances and fittings to be carried out at least once every twelve months. The inspection must be carried out by someone who is registered with Gas Safety Register. Their website is: www.gassaferegister.co.uk. The landlord must also keep a record of the date of the check, any problems identified and any action taken. As the tenant, you have the right to see this record as long as you give reasonable notice.

If your landlord does not arrange for checks or refuses to allow you to see the record of the check, you could contact the local Health and Safety Executive office.

The right to stay in the accommodation

This is an outline of the rights you have as a tenant of a local authority, housing association or housing co-operative to stay in your accommodation and how you can be evicted.

Secure tenants

As a secure tenant you have the right to stay in the accommodation as long as you keep to the terms of the tenancy agreement with your landlord. However, if the tenancy agreement is broken, for example, because of rent arrears or nuisance to neighbours, your landlord can serve a notice on you and apply to the county court for eviction.

A social housing landlord can only evict you if they give you the proper notice and if one of the 'grounds for possession' applies.

What constitutes 'grounds for possession' is complicated and someone whose landlord is seeking eviction should consult an experienced adviser, for example, at a Citizens Advice Bureau.

The landlord must apply to the county court to seek possession of the property and a secure tenant can only be evicted if the court grants a possession order to the landlord.

Assured tenants

As an assured tenant you have the right to stay in the accommodation as long as you keep to the terms of the tenancy agreement with your landlord. However, if the tenancy agreement is broken, for example, because of rent arrears or nuisance to neighbours, your landlord can serve a notice on you.

The housing association will then have to obtain a possession order from the county court by proving that one of the 'grounds for possession' applies. We discussed grounds for possession earlier in the book.

Social housing tenancies and discrimination

When renting accommodation from a local authority, housing association or other social landlord, they must not discriminate against you because of your disability, gender reassignment, pregnancy and maternity, race, religion or belief, sex or sexual orientation. This means that they are not allowed to:

- rent a property to you on worse terms than other tenants
- treat you differently from other tenants in the way you are allowed to use facilities such as a laundry or a garden
- evict or harass you because of discrimination
- charge you higher rent than other tenants
- refuse to re-house you because of discrimination
- refuse to carry out repairs to your home because of disrimination
- refuse to make reasonable changes to a property or a term in the tenancy agreement which would allow a disabled person to live there.

If you think your landlord is discriminating against you, you should get advice from an experienced adviser, for example, at a Citizens Advice Bureau.

Introductory tenants -who is an introductory tenant?
Some local authorities make all new tenants introductory tenants for the first 12 months of the tenancy.

Rights of introductory tenants
Introductory tenants have some but not all of the rights of secure tenants. The following table shows your rights as an introductory tenant compared with secure tenants.

Statutory right	Secure tenant	Introductory tenant
Right to succession by partners or in some cases family members	yes	yes
Right to repair	yes	yes
Right to assign	yes	no
Right to buy	yes	no, but period spent as an introductory tenant counts towards the discount
Right to take in lodgers	yes	no
Right to sub-let part of your home	yes	no
Right to do improvements	yes	no
Right to exchange your home with certain other tenants	yes	no
Right to vote prior to transfer to new landlord	yes	no
Right to be consulted on housing management issues	yes	yes
Right to be consulted on decision to delegate housing management	yes	yes
Right to participate in housing management contract monitoring	yes	yes

Ending an introductory tenancy

At the end of the twelve months, provided there have been no possession proceedings against you, the introductory tenancy will usually be converted by your landlord to a secure tenancy. However, your landlord may decide to extend the introductory tenancy for a further six months. If this happens, you will be told the reasons for the decision and given the chance to ask for the decision to be reviewed.

Possession proceedings

It is very easy for a landlord to evict an introductory tenant. If you have received a notice from the landlord stating that they intend to evict you and take possession of the property, you should immediately consult an experienced adviser, for example, at a Citizens Advice Bureau.

Flexible tenants

Flexible tenancies are a type of tenancy that can be granted by local authority landlords in England, from 1 April 2012. Not all local authorities offer them.

A flexible tenancy is similar to a local authority secure tenancy. However, a secure tenancy is periodic, which means that it lasts for an indefinite period of time. Periodic tenancies are often called 'lifetime tenancies'. In contrast, a flexible tenancy lasts for a fixed period of time. In most cases, a flexible tenancy will last for at least five years.

A local authority has to serve a written notice on you before a flexible tenancy can start. The notice must tell you that the tenancy you're being offered is a flexible tenancy, and what the terms of the tenancy are.

Flexible tenants have a number of legal rights, many of which are similar to the rights of secure tenants. For example, the right to pass on your tenancy when you're alive or when you die, the right to exchange your home with certain other tenants, and the right to buy your home.

A local authority doesn't have to grant you another tenancy when the fixed term of the flexible tenancy comes to an end. You can ask the local authority to review its decision not to grant you another tenancy. The review will consider if your landlord has followed its policies and procedures when making that decision.

If you are not given another tenancy when your flexible tenancy comes to an end, the local authority will take action to evict you.

****

Ch. 11

Private Tenancies in Scotland

The law governing the relationship between private landlords and tenants in Scotland is different to that in England. Since the beginning of 1989, new private sector tenancies in Scotland have been covered by the Housing (Scotland) Act 1988. Following the passage of this Act, private sector tenants no longer have any protection as far as rent levels are concerned and tenants enjoy less security of tenure. However, **The Private Housing (Tenancies) (Scotland) Act 2016**, passed by the Scottish Parliament and coming into force at the end of 2017 may have some bearing in this area. The main provisions of the Act are outlined at the end of this chapter.

Short assured and assured tenancies
Most residential lettings in Scotland made after 2 January 1989 are short assured tenancies. Those that aren't short assured are normally assured tenancies.

Short assured tenancies
This is the most common type of tenancy. A short assured tenancy makes it easier for a landlord to get a property than an assured tenancy. Before any agreement is signed, a landlord must use form AT5 to tell new tenants that the tenancy will be a short assured tenancy. (see appendix). If they don't, the tenancy will automatically

be an assured tenancy. Initially, a short assured tenancy must be for 6 months or more. After the first 6 months, the tenancy can be renewed for a shorter period.

Assured tenancies

At the beginning of an assured tenancy, it will be classed as a 'contractual assured tenancy' for a fixed period of time. The tenancy automatically becomes a 'statutory assured tenancy' if:

- the landlord ends the tenancy by issuing a notice to quit (eg because they want to change the agreement) and the tenant stays in the property
- the fixed period covered by the tenancy comes to an end and the tenant stays in the property

There are different rights and responsibilities on both landlord and tenant depending on the type of assured tenancy.

Other types of tenancy

Most tenancies in Scotland are short assured or assured tenancies. The other tenancy types are:

- 'common law' tenancy - if a tenant shares their home as a lodger
- regulated tenancy - the most common form of tenancy before 1989
- agricultural tenancy
- crofting tenancy

'Common law' tenancies

If a landlord is sharing their house or flat with their tenants, they can't use the short assured or assured tenancy. Instead, they will automatically have what is known as a 'common law tenancy'. The tenant doesn't have to have a written contract but the landlord may use a lodger agreement to create a contract between them and the tenant - so both are clear about what has been agreed. (see appendix for sample lodger agreement).

Regulated tenancies

Tenancies created before 2 January 1989 are generally regulated tenancies. As not many exist we will not be describing them further here.

Agricultural tenancies

There are 3 types of agricultural tenancy:

- limited duration tenancy - if the lease is for more than 5 years
- short limited duration tenancy - if the lease is for 5 years or less
- 1991 Act tenancy - if the tenancy began before 2003

All agricultural tenants have the right to:

- a written lease
- compensation at the end of the tenancy for any improvements they made to the land during your tenancy
- leave the tenancy to a spouse or relative in their will

If the lease is over 5 years, agricultural tenants can also:

- pass their tenancy on to a relative or spouse within their lifetime
- use the land for non-agricultural purposes
- Tenants with a 1991 Act tenancy have the right to buy the land they are leasing.

If there's a house on the land, both landlord and tenant have obligations to keep it in good repair.

Crofting tenancies

Crofting is a system of landholding unique to the Highlands and Islands of Scotland. Usually, the crofter holds the croft on the 'statutory conditions' and doesn't have a written lease. Crofting is regulated by the Crofting Commission. You must get written agreement from the Commission if you want to make any changes to a crofting tenancy (including a change of tenant).

What the landlord must include in a tenancy agreement

If a landlord uses an assured or short assured tenancy, the agreement must be written down. It must include:

- the names of all people involved
- the rental price and how it's paid
- the deposit amount and how it will be protected (see below)
- when the deposit can be fully or partly withheld (eg to repair damage caused by tenants)

- the property address
- the start and end date of the tenancy
- any tenant or landlord obligations
- who's responsible for minor repairs
- which bills your tenants are responsible for
- a statement telling the tenant that antisocial behaviour is a breach of the agreement

For other types of tenancy, it's still good practice to put the agreement in writing.

ncluding other information

To avoid any confusion later, the landlord can include other information in the agreement, such as:

- whether the tenancy can be ended early and how this can be done
- information on how and when the rent will be reviewed
- whether the property can be let to someone else (sublet) or have lodgers

Changes to tenancy agreements

The landlord must get the agreement of their tenants if they want to make changes to the terms of their tenancy agreement.

Preventing discrimination

Unless the landlord have a very strong reason, they must change anything in a tenancy agreement that might discriminate against tenants on the grounds of:

- gender
- sexual orientation
- disability (or because of something connected with their disability)
- religion or belief
- being a transsexual person
- the tenant being pregnant or having a baby

Ending a tenancy

Tenancies don't automatically end when the term of the tenancy agreement comes to an end. To end a tenancy agreement, the landlord must follow the correct procedures starting with a Notice to quit. To end any tenancy other than a common law tenancy, a landlord must give tenants a 'notice to quit'. Even for common law tenancies, this is still good practice. Landlords don't have to use a particular form, but for a notice to quit to be valid it must be in writing and must tell tenants:

- how much notice the landlord is giving them
- that the landlord still needs a court order to get their property back if the tenants don't leave when the notice runs out
- that the tenant can get independent advice about the notice - and where they can get that advice from)

Short assured tenancy

To get a property back, the landlord must give tenants a 'notice to quit' and a 'Section 33 notice'. For a short assured tenancy, the

103

minimum notice period is 40 days if the tenancy is for 6 months or longer.

For a tenancy that is continuing on a month by month basis after the original period has ended, the notice period is a minimum of 28 days. The landlord must give 2 months notice when giving a Section 33 notice. They can issue both the notice to quit and Section 33 notice at the same time. (see appendix)

Other tenancy types

For other tenancy types the landlord must give at least:

- 28 days if the tenancy is for up to 1 month
- 31 days if the tenancy is for up to 3 months
- 40 days if the tenancy is for more than 3 months

Ending a tenancy early

A landlord can end a tenancy early if:

- the tenant breaks a condition of the tenancy agreement
- landlord and tenant agree to end the tenancy

If tenants don't leave

If the notice period expires and tenants don't leave the property, the landlord can start the process of eviction through the courts. A landlord must tell tenants of their intention to get a court order by giving them a 'notice of intention to raise proceedings' (AT6) (see appendix).

If tenants want to leave

The tenancy agreement should say how much notice tenants need to give before they can leave the property. If the notice isn't mentioned in the tenancy agreement, the minimum notice a tenant can give is:

- 28 days if their tenancy runs on a month-to-month basis (or if it's for less than a month)
- 40 days if their tenancy is for longer than 3 months

Ending a tenancy early

Unless there's a break clause in the tenancy agreement, a landlord can insist that their tenants pay rent until the end of the tenancy. If tenants leave the property without giving notice, or before the notice has run out, they're still responsible for the property and the rent by law.

Houses in multiple occupation (HMOs)

If you are living in a bedsit, shared flat, lodging, shared house, hostel or bed and breakfast accommodation it's likely that you'll be living a house in multiple occupation or 'HMO'. It's likely that you live in an HMO if:

- you live with two or more other people, and
- you don't belong to the same family, and
- you share some facilities, e.g. a bathroom or kitchen, and
- the accommodation is your only or main home (if you are a student, your term-time residence counts as your main home).

If you live with a homeowner their family don't count as 'qualifying persons' when deciding whether or not a property is an HMO. So for example, if you share accommodation with the owner and one other unrelated lodger, you won't live in an HMO. If you live with the owner and two other unrelated lodgers, you will live in an HMO. Before the council gives a landlord an HMO licence, it will carry out the following checks:

Is the landlord is a fit and proper person to hold a licence?

Before it will grant an HMO licence, the council must check that the owner and anyone who manages the property (for example, a letting agent) don't have any criminal convictions, for example, for fraud or theft.

Is the property managed properly?

The council must check that your landlord respects your legal rights as a tenant. You should be given a written tenancy agreement stating clearly what your landlord's responsibilities are, and what your responsibilities are. This should cover things like rent, repairs and other rules. To manage the property properly, your landlord must:

- keep the property and any furniture and fittings in good repair
- deal with you fairly and legally when it comes to rent and other payments, for example they:
- must go through the correct procedure if they want to increase your rent
- cannot resell you gas or electricity at a profit

- not evict you illegally
- make sure that their tenants don't annoy or upset other people living in the area.

Does the property meet the required standards?

To meet the standards expected of an HMO property:

- the rooms must be a decent size, for example, every bedroom should be able to accommodate a bed, a wardrobe and a chest of drawers.
- there must be enough kitchen and bathroom facilities for the number of people living in the property, with adequate hot and cold water supplies.
- adequate fire safety measures must be installed, for example your landlord must provide smoke alarms and self-closing fire doors and make sure there is an emergency escape route.
- all gas and electrical appliances must be safe.
- heating, lighting and ventilation must all be adequate.
- the property should be secure, with good locks on the doors and windows.
- there must be a phone line installed so that tenants can set up a contract with a phone company to supply the service.

What are my landlord's responsibilities?

In order to keep their HMO licence, your landlord must maintain the property properly:

- Common parts - these must be kept clean and in good repair (for example, the stairwell, hall, shared kitchen and bathroom). However, the landlord can include a clause in the tenancy agreement which passes this responsibility onto the tenants.

- **Shared facilities** - these should be kept in good repair (for example, the cooker, boiler, fridge, sinks, bath and lighting)
- **Heating, hot water and ventilation** - these facilities must all be kept in good order
- **Gas safety** - all gas appliances and installations must be safe (for example, a gas fire, boiler or cooker) - these should be checked once a year by a Gas Safe Register engineer
- **Electrical safety** - all electrical appliances and installations must be safe - these should be tested every three years by a contractor approved by the National Inspection Council for Electrical Installation Contracting (NICEIC) or SELECT, Scotland's trade association for the electrical, electronics and communications systems industry
- **Fire precautions** - all fire precautions (for example, smoke alarms and fire extinguishers) must be in good working order and that the fire escape route is kept safe and free from obstructions
- **Furniture** - all furniture supplied must meet safety standards (for example, isn't flammable)
- **Roof, windows and exterior** - these must all be adequately maintained
- **Rubbish** - enough rubbish bins must be provided
- **Deposits** - your deposit must be returned within a reasonable time when you move out, preferably within 14 days.

Your landlord should also put up notices in the accommodation:

- giving the name and address of the person responsible for managing it so that you can contact them whenever necessary
- explaining what you should do in an emergency, for example if there is a gas leak or a fire.

Tenants responsibilities:

- **Repairs** - you should let your landlord know if anything in the property needs repairing, particularly if this is something they are responsible for keeping in good order, such as the roof, boiler or toilet
- **Damage** - you must take good care of the property and try not to damage anything
- **Rubbish** - not let rubbish pile up in or around the property but dispose of it properly in the bins provided
- **Inspections** - let the landlord inspect the property so they can check whether any maintenance work needs doing. Normally this should happen once every six months. Your landlord must give you 24 hours' written notice before coming round.
- **Behave responsibly** - make sure that you don't behave in a way that can annoy or upset your neighbours. Your landlord is responsible for dealing with any complaints made by your neighbours and must take action if they are unhappy with your behaviour.

If you don't think your landlord is managing the property properly and maintaining these standards, there are two steps you can take:

- talk to your landlord - they may not realise that there is a problem until you discuss it with them.
- tell your local council - they have powers to make your landlord bring the management and physical conditions of the HMO up to standard.

Usually, the council department responsible for HMOs is the environmental health department. Contact your local council to talk to an environmental health officer about your complaint. If you don't want your landlord to know that you have complained, let the officer know, and they will then keep your complaint in the strictest confidence.

If you have an assured, short assured or regulated tenancy or you live in tied accommodation, you can report your landlord to the The Housing and Property Chamber of the First Tier Tribunal if you believe your home doesn't meet the repairing standard.

Safeguarding Tenancy Deposits
A tenancy deposit scheme is a scheme provided by an independent third party to protect deposits until they are due to be repaid. Three schemes are now operating:
- Letting Protection Service Scotland
- Safedeposits Scotland
- Mydeposits Scotland

Landlord's legal duties
The legal duties on landlords who receive a tenancy deposit are:

- to pay deposits to an approved tenancy deposit scheme
- to provide the tenant with key information about the tenancy and deposit

Key dates for landlords
The dates by which landlords must pay deposits to an approved scheme and provide information to the tenant vary, depending on when the deposit was received:

1. Deposit received prior to 7 March 2011:
Where the tenancy is renewed by express agreement or tacit relocation on or after 2 October 2012 and before 2 April 2013 (Regulation 47(a))
Within 30 working days of renewal. In any other case by 15 May 2013

2. Deposit received on or after 7 March 2011 and before 2 July 2012
By 13 November 2012

3. Deposit received on or after 2 July 2012 and before 2 October 2012
By 13 November 2012

4. Deposit received on or after 2 October 2012
Within 30 working days of the beginning of the tenancy
Information about the schemes
Further details about the individual schemes are available on the individual scheme web sites below. Email addresses and telephone

numbers are also included. All three schemes have a range of information available for both landlords (and their agents) as well as tenants and these include how landlords can join the schemes, how to submit deposits, how to ask for repayment of deposits and how the dispute resolution service will work.

Letting Protection Service Scotland
www.lettingprotectionscotland.com
Address:
The Pavilions
Bridgwater Road
Bristol
BS99 6BN
Email contact: events@lettingprotectionscotland.com
Telephone: 0330 303 0031

SafeDeposits Scotland
www.safedepositsscotland.com
Address:
Lower Ground
250 West George Street
Glasgow
G2 4QY
Email contact: info@safedepositsscotland.com
Telephone: 03333 213 136

Mydeposits Scotland
www.mydepositsscotland.co.uk
Address:

Premiere House
Elstree Way
Borehamwood
Hertfordshire
WD6 1JH
Email contact: info@mydepositsscotland.co.uk
Telephone: 0333 321 9402

****

Ch. 12

Relationship Breakdown and Housing Rights

When a relationship breaks down, whether the people in question are married or not, problems can often occur in relation to the property that was home. The rights of people will depend mainly on whether they are married or not, whether they are in a civil partnership or whether there are children involved and the legal status of individuals in the home.

Housing rights in an emergency

In the main, it is women who suffer from domestic violence. This section refers to women but the rights are the same for men. If you are a woman, and have been threatened by a man and are forced to leave your home then there are several possibilities for action in an emergency. The first of these is either going to a women's refuge. These provide shelter, advice and emotional support for women and children. These refuges will always try to admit you and as a result are sometimes crowded. They will always try to find you somewhere to live in the longer term. Refuges have a 24-hour telephone service if you need to find somewhere. For addresses see *useful addresses* at the back of this book.

Approaching the council

A person suffering domestic violence who has been forced to flee can approach the local council and ask for help as a homeless person.

Councils will demand proof of violence and you will need to get evidence from a professional person, such as doctor or social worker or police. The council decides whether or not it has a duty to help you and you should seek advice if they refuse. Some councils, but not all will offer help to battered women. If you are accepted as homeless then the council should not send you back to the area where the violence began.

Obtaining a court order

Another course of action in an emergency is to obtain a court order against the man you live with.

Courts can issue orders stating that a man:

- should not assault you or harass you
- not to assault any children living with you
- to leave the home and not to return
- to keep a certain distance from your home or any other place where your children go regularly.
- to let you back in your home if you have been excluded.

If you believe a court order would help, you should get advice on where to find a solicitor or law centre that deals with these types of applications to the court. Certain orders are harder to get than others, such as exclusion orders. Matters need to be very serious indeed before such an order will be made. However, you will be advised of this when approaching a solicitor or law centre. Failure to obey the terms and conditions laid down in the order can lead to arrest for contempt and a fine or even imprisonment.

Long-term rights to the home

Long-term rights to stay in a home depend on a number of circumstances. If you are married or in a civil partnership and the ownership or tenancy of the property is in joint names you have equal rights to live in the property. If it is owned then you will have a right to a share of the proceeds if it is sold. In certain circumstances you have a right to more (or less) than a half share, or to the tenancy in your name after divorce.

If you are married or in a civil partnership but the ownership or tenancy is in one name only there are laws to protect the rights of the other party. Courts have the power to decide who has the ownership or rights over the matrimonial home, even if the property is held in one persons name only. This can also apply to people who were married but are now divorced and to those who were planning to get married within three years of their engagement.

Spouses who are not the owner or tenant of the home have a right to stay there. The court has the power to exclude either of the spouses, even if they are sole or joint owner or tenant. If your husband has left and stopped paying the rent or mortgage payments, the landlord or building society is obliged to accept payments from you, if you wish to make them, even if the property is not in your name. If the home is owned by your husband then you can register your right to live in it. This prevents your husband selling the home before the court has decided who should live there. And also prevents him taking out a second mortgage on the property without your knowledge. This is known as 'registering a charge' on the home. The court also has the power to transfer a fully protected private tenancy, an assured tenancy or a council or housing association tenancy from one partner to another.

If the matrimonial home is owner occupied and proceedings have started for a divorce, the court will decide how the value of the property will be divided up. The law recognises that, even if the property is in the husbands/civil partners name only, the wife/civil partner has a right to a share in its value, that she/he often makes a large unpaid contribution through housework or looking after children and that this should be recognised in divorce proceedings. The court looks at a number of things when reaching a decision:

- the income and resources of both partners
- the needs of you and your husband
- the standard of living that you and your husband had before the breakdown
- ages of partners and length of marriage/civil partnership
- contributions to the welfare of the family
- conduct of partners
- loss of benefits that you might have had if the marriage/civil partnership had not broken down.

The court also has to consider whether there is any way that they can make a 'clean break' between you and your husband/civil partner so that there are no further financial ties between you. In certain circumstances, the court can order sale of the matrimonial home and the distribution of proceeds between partners.

If you are not married or in a Civil Partnership

If you are not married/in a civil partnership then your rights will depend on who is the tenant or the owner of the home.

Tenants

If a tenancy is in joint names then you both have equal rights to the home. You can exclude your partner temporarily as we have seen by a court order. If you are a council tenant then you may want to see if you can get the council to rehouse you. You should get advice on this from an independent agency (see useful addresses).

If the tenancy is in your partners name only then the other person can apply for the right to stay there, for their partner to be excluded or for the tenancy to be transferred.

Home owners

If you live in an owner occupied property you and you partner may have certain rights to a share of the property even if you are not married/in a civil partnership.

If the home is jointly owned then you have a clear right to a share in its value. If one person has contributed more than the other then a court can decide that an equal share is unfair. The court cannot order the transfer of the ownership of property but it can order the sale and distribution of the proceeds.

If the home is in one persons name there is no automatic right to live in the home, even if there are children. However, a solicitor acting on your behalf can argue that by virtue of marriage/civil partnership and contribution you should be allowed to stay there and be entitled to a share.

****

Ch. 13

Housing Advice

General advice

Citizens Advice Bureaus, which are situated throughout the U.K., provide advice on all problems, including housing and other matters such as legal, welfare benefits and relationship breakdown. If appropriate they can refer you for more specialist help to a solicitor or advice agency. This advice is free of charge. To find a local office, look in the telephone directory under National Association of Citizens Advice Bureau.

Housing Advice Centres

In many areas there are specialist advice centres offering housing aid and advice. The service they offer varies from one-off information to detailed help over a long period.

There are two main types of housing advice centres, Local council housing aid centres which can advise on all kinds of problems, although they will not be able to take action against their own council. Independent housing aid centres may be better equipped to do this. These centres can offer detailed assistance over a length of time and also one-off advice. There are a number of independent housing aid centres throughout the country operated by Shelter. You should contact Shelter for your nearest centre.

Other specialist advice

Law centers-they offer free advice and can sometimes represent you in court. They can usually advise on all aspects of law and also advise battered women. They cannot, however, take divorce cases. For this you will need a solicitor. Shelter can provide a list of law centers.

For advice on welfare rights you should try the local council, who may employ a welfare rights advisor. Advisers can also contact the advice line which is run by the Child Poverty Action Group. For women's rights the Women's Aid Federation England and Welsh Women's Aid refer battered women, with or without children, to refuges. They can put you in touch with sympathetic solicitors and local women's aid groups and can offer a range of other advice, such as welfare benefits.

For immigration advice, the Joint Council for the Welfare of Immigrants offers advice on all types of problems connected with immigration and nationality. The United Kingdom Immigrants Advisory Service offers advice and help on problems with immigration. The Refugee Council has an advice service for refugees and asylum seekers.

Advice from solicitors

Solicitors can advise you on all aspects of the law, represent you in certain courts and, if necessary, get a barrister to represent you. It is best to find a solicitor who specialises in housing rights as they usually have a wider knowledge of specific areas. You can get a list of solicitors who specialise in housing law from the Community Legal Service (CLS) Directory in your local library. The list is also on the

CLS website. Citizens Advice Bureaus can also supply specialist solicitor details.

Free advice and help

The Legal Help Scheme, whilst also being squeezed, can pay for up to two hours worth of free advice and assistance and for matrimonial cases up to three hours. The scheme is means tested and you must come within the limits of the scheme to qualify. For details of the scheme you should approach a Citizens Advice Bureau or a solicitors practice operating the scheme. You must have reasonable grounds for defending an action. In certain cases, if you succeed in obtaining cash compensation then you may have to pay a proportion of it back, this is known as the *statutory charge*

****

GLOSSARY

FREEHOLDER: Someone who owns their property outright.

LEASEHOLDER: Someone who has been granted permission to live on someone else's land for a fixed term.

TENANCY: One form of lease, the most common types of which are fixed-term or periodic.

LANDLORD: A person who owns the property in which the tenant lives.

LICENCE: A licence is an agreement entered into whereby the landlord is merely giving you permission to occupy his/her property for a limited period of time.

TRESPASSER: Someone who has no right through an agreement to live in a property.

PROTECTED TENANT: In the main, subject to certain exclusions, someone whose tenancy began before 15th January 1989.

ASSURED TENANT: In the main, subject to certain exclusions, someone whose tenancy began after 15th January 1989.

NOTICE TO QUIT: A legal document giving the protected tenant twenty eight days notice that the landlord intends to apply for possession of the property to the County Court.

GROUND FOR POSSESSION: One of the stated reasons for which the landlord can apply for possession of the property.

MANDATORY GROUND: Where the judge must give possession of the property.

DISCRETIONARY GROUND: Where the judge may or may not give possession, depending on his own opinion.

STUDENT LETTING: A tenancy granted by a specified educational institution.

HOLIDAY LETTING: A dwelling used for holiday purposes only.

ASSURED SHORTHOLD TENANCY: A fixed-term post-1989 tenancy.

PAYMENT OF RENT: Where you pay a regular sum of money in return for permission to occupy a property or land for a specified period of time.

FAIR RENT: A rent set by the Rent Officer every two years for most pre-1989 tenancies and which is lower than a market rent.

MARKET RENT: A rent deemed to be comparable with other non-fair rents in the area.

RENT ASSESSMENT COMMITTEE: A committee set up to review rents set by either the Rent Officer or the landlord.

PREMIUM: A sum of money charged for permission to live in a property.

DEPOSIT: A sum of money held against the possibility of damage to property.

QUIET ENJOYMENT: The right to live peacefully in your own Home.

REPAIRS: Work required to keep a property in good order.

IMPROVEMENTS: Alterations to a property.

LEGAL AID: Help with your legal costs, which is dependent on income.

HOUSING BENEFIT: Financial help with rent, which is dependent on income.

HOUSING ADVICE CENTRE: A center which exists to give advice on housing-related matters and which is usually local authority-funded.

LAW CENTRE: A center, which exists for the purpose of assisting the public with legal advice.

Appendix 1 – Useful addresses

Age UK
Tavis House
1-6 Tavistock Square
London WC1 9NA
0800 169 8787
www.ageuk.org.uk

Child Poverty Action Group
30 Micawber Street
London N1 7TB
020 7837 7979

Consumers Association
2 Marylebone Road
London NW1 4DF
01992 822 800
www.which.co.uk

Disability Rights
Ground Floor
CAN Mezzanine
49-51 East Rd
London
N1 6AH tel: 0207 250 8181

Gay and Lesbian Switchboard
0300 330 0630
switchboard.lgbt

Homeless Link
8 Milverton Street
London SE11 4AP
020 7840 4430
www.homeless.org.uk

Immigration Advisory Service
iasservices.org

Generation Rent
Unit E03, The Biscuit Factory,
100 Clements Road,
London SE16 4DG
www.generationrent.org

Leasehold Advisory Service
0207 832 2500
www.lease-advice.org.uk

Legal Action Group
48 Chancery Lane
London
WC2A 1JF
020 7833 2931
www.lag.org.uk

Liberty (Council for Civil Liberties)
Liberty House,
26-30 Strutton Ground,

London, SW1P 2HR
0207 403 3888
www.liberty-humanrights.org.uk

Shelter
Housing and Homeless Charity
0808 800 4444 (advice helpline)
www.england.shelter.org.uk

Women's Aid Federation Helpline
0808 2000 247
www.womensaid.org.uk

****

Appendix

Sample Assured Shorthold Tenancy Agreement (England and Wales)

Sample Section 21 Notice Requiring possession (FORM 6A)

Notes to Form 6A

Sample tenancy agreement (Scotland)

Sample Notices Scotland (AT5)
(NTQ) (S33) (AT6)

Sample lodger agreement (Can be used in Scotland or England and Wales)

Sample Landlords Inventory

ASSURED SHORTHOLD TENANCY AGREEMENT ENGLAND AND WALES

This Tenancy Agreement is between

Name and address of Landlord-
-AND

Name of tenant:

Tenant"

(in the case of Joint Tenants the term "Tenant" applies to each of them and the names of all Joint Tenants should be written above. Each Tenant individually has the full responsibilities and rights set out in this Agreement)

Address-in respect of:

("the Premises")

Description of Premises
-Which comprises of:
Term-The Tenancy is granted for a fixed term of [6] months

Date of start of tenancy-The Tenancy begins on:

("The Commencement Date") and is an assured shorthold monthly tenancy, the terms of which are set out in this Agreement.

Overcrowding-The Tenant agrees not to allow any person other than the Tenant to reside at the Premises.

Payment of Deposit-The Tenant agrees to pay on signing the Agreement a deposit of

£   which will be returnable in full providing that the Landlord may deduct from such sums: The reasonable costs of any necessary repairs to the premises, building or common parts, or the replacement of any or all of the contents where such repair or replacement is due to any act or omission of the Tenant or family or visitors of the Tenant, such sums as are outstanding on leaving the Premises in respect of arrears or other charges including Court costs or other fees.

The deposit will be protected by The Deposit Protection Service (The DPS) in accordance with the Terms and Conditions of The DPS. The Terms and Conditions and ADR Rules governing the protection of the deposit including the repayment process can be found at www.depositprotection.com

Payment for the premises-
Rent: The rent for the premises is:

Service Charge:
Total:

In this Agreement the term "Rent" refers to the net rent and service charge set out above or as varied from time to time in accordance with this Agreement. The payment of monthly Rent is due in advance on the first Saturday of each month.

The service charge is in respect of the landlord providing the services listed in Schedule 1 to this Agreement for which the Tenant shall pay a service charge to be included in the rent. The service charge may be varied by the landlord in accordance with the terms set out in Schedule 1 to this Agreement.

I/We have read, understood and accept the terms and conditions contained within this agreement which include the standard terms and conditions attached.

Signed by the Tenant

.... Dated:

Signed on behalf of the landlord
....,,,,,,,,,, Dated·

If the Tenant feels that the landlord has broken this Agreement or not performed any obligation contained in it, he/she should first complain to the landlord in writing giving details of the breach or non-performance.

Terms and Conditions

1. It is agreed that:
Changes in Rent-1.1-The landlord may increase or decrease the Rent by giving the Tenant not less than 4 weeks notice in writing of the

increase or decrease. The notice shall specify the Rent proposed. The first increase or decrease shall be on the first day of   following the Commencement Date of this Agreement. Subsequent increases or decreases in the Rent shall take effect on the first day of   in each subsequent year. The revised Rent shall be the amount specified in the notice of increase unless the Tenant exercises his/her right to refer the notice to a Rent Assessment Committee to have a market rent determined in which case the maximum Rent payable for one year after the date specified in the notice shall be the Rent so determined.

Altering the Agreement-1.2-With the exception of any changes in Rent, this Agreement may only be altered by the agreement in writing of both the Tenant and the landlord.

2. The landlord agrees:

Possession-2.1-To give the Tenant possession of the Premises at the commencement of the Tenancy.

Tenant's Right to Occupy-2.2-Not to interrupt or interfere with the Tenant's right peacefully to occupy the Premises except where:

(i)   access is required to inspect the condition of the Premises or to carry out repairs or other works to the Premises or adjoining property; or

(ii)   a court has given the Association possession by ending the Tenancy.

Repair of Structure and Exterior- 2.3-To keep in good repair the structure and exterior of the Premises including:

(i)   drains, gutters and external pipes;

(ii)   the roof;

(iii)   outside wall, outside doors, windowsills, window catches, sash cords and window frames including necessary external painting and decorating;

(iv)   internal walls, floors and ceilings, doors and door frames, door hinges and skirting boards but not including internal painting and decoration;

(v)   plasterwork;

(vi)   chimneys, chimney stacks and flues but not including sweeping;

(vii)   pathways, steps or other means of access;

(viii)   integral garages and stores;

(ix)   boundary walls and fences.

Repair of Installations- 2.4-To keep in good repair and working order any installations provided by the landlord for space heating, water heating and sanitation and for the supply of water, gas and electricity including:

(i)   basins, sinks, baths, toilets, flushing systems and waste pipes;

(ii)   electric wiring including sockets and switches, gas pipes and water pipes;

(III)   water heaters, fireplaces, fitted fires and central heating installations

Repair of Common Parts- 2.5-To take reasonable care to keep the common entrances, halls, stairways, lifts, passageways, rubbish chutes and any other common parts, including their lighting, in reasonable repair and fit for use by the Tenant and other occupiers and visitors to the Premises.

External & Internal
Decorations-2.6-To keep the exterior and interior of the Premises and any common parts in a good state of decoration and normally to decorate these areas once every 5 years.

3. The Tenant agrees:

Possession-3.1-To take possession of the Premises at the commencement of the Tenancy and not to part with possession of the Premises or sub-let the whole or part of it.

Rent-3.2-To pay the Rent monthly and in advance. The first payment shall be made on the signing of the Agreement in respect of the period from the Commencement Date to the first Saturday of the following month.

Use of Premises- 3.3-To use the Premises for residential purposes as the Tenant's only or principal home and not to operate a business at the Premises without the written consent of the landlord.

Nuisance and Racial and other Harassment- 3.4-Not to behave or allow members of his/her household or any other person visiting the Premises with the Tenant's permission to behave in a manner nor do anything which is likely to be a nuisance to the tenants, owners or lessees of any of the other properties or other persons lawfully visiting the property. In particular, not to cause any interference, nuisance or annoyance through noise, anti-social behaviour or threats of or actual violence or any damage to property belonging to the said persons. This Clause also applies to any conduct or activity which amounts to harassment including: abuse and intimidation, creating unacceptable levels of noise or causing intentional damage or any other persistent behaviour which causes offence, discomfort or inconvenience on the grounds of colour, race religion, sex, sexual orientation and disability.

Noise-3.5-Not to play or allow to be played any radio, television, audio equipment or musical instrument so loudly that it causes a nuisance or annoyance to neighbours or can be heard outside the Premises.

Domestic Violence- 3.6-Not to use or threaten violence against any other person living in the Premises such that they are forced to leave by reason of the Tenant's violence or fear of such violence.

Pets-3.7-To keep under control any animals at the Premises and to obtain the written consent of the landlord before keeping a dog or any other animal.

Car Repairs-3.8-That no car servicing or car repairs shall be carried out in the roads or accessway or parking spaces or in the forecourt or approaches to the Premises, such as to be a nuisance or annoyance to neighbours.

Paraffin-3.9-Not to use any paraffin or bottled gas heating, lighting or cooking appliances on the Premises nor any appliances which discharge the products of combustion into the interior of the Premises.

Vehicles-3.10-That no commercial vehicle, caravan, boat, or lorry shall be parked in the accessway or parking spaces (regardless of whether this forms part of the Premises) or in the forecourt or approaches to the Premises or the adjoining premises.

Keeping premises clean-3.11-To keep the interior of the Premises in a clean condition. The Tenant agrees to return the property in the same decorative order as at the start of the tenancy taking into account fair wear and tear.

Damage-3.12-To make good any damage caused wilfully or by neglect or carelessness on the part of the Tenant or any member of the Tenant's household or visitor to the Premises including the replacement of any broken glass in windows and repair or replacement of any damaged fittings and installations. If the Tenant fails to make good any damage for which he/she is responsible the landlord may enter the Premises and carry out the work in default and the cost of this work shall be recoverable by the Association from the Tenant.

Reporting Disrepair- 3.13-To report to the landlord any disrepair or defect for which the landlord is responsible in the structure or exterior of the Premises or in any installation therein or in the common parts.

Access-3.14-To allow the landlords employees or contractors acting on behalf of the landlord access at all reasonable hours of the daytime to inspect the condition of the Premises or to carry out repairs or other works to the Premises or adjoining property. The landlord will normally give at least 24 hours' notice, but immediate access may be required and shall be given in an emergency.

Assignment- 3.15-Not to assign the Tenancy.

Sub-Tenants- 3.16-Not to sub-let the whole or part of the Premises.

Ending the Tenancy- 3.17-To give the landlord at least [4   ] weeks notice in writing when the Tenant wishes to end the Tenancy.

Moving Out- 3.18-To give the landlord vacant possession and return the keys of the Premises at the end of the Tenancy and to remove all personal possessions and rubbish and leave the Premises and the landlords furniture and fixtures in good lettable condition and repair. The landlord accepts no responsibility for anything left at the Premises by the Tenant at the end of the Tenancy.

4. The Tenant has the following rights:

Right to Occupy- 4.1-The Tenant has the right to occupy the Premises without interruption or interference from the landlord for the duration of this Tenancy (except for the obligation contained in this Agreement to give access to the landlords employees or contractors) so long as the Tenant complies with the terms of this Agreement and has proper respect for the rights of other tenants and neighbours.

Security of Tenure- 4.2-The Tenant has security of tenure as an assured tenant so long as he/she occupies the Premises as his/her only or principal home. Before the expiry of the fixed term the landlord can only end the Tenancy by obtaining a court order for possession of the Premises on one of the grounds listed in Schedule 2 of the Housing Act 1988. The landlord will only use the following grounds to obtain an order for possession

--The tenant has not paid rent which is due; (Ground 10)
The Tenant has broken, or failed to perform, any of the conditions of this Tenancy; (Ground 12)
The Tenant or anyone living in the premises has caused damage to, or failed to look after the premises, the building, any of the common parts; (Ground 13)
The Tenant or anyone living in the premises has caused serious or persistent nuisance or annoyance to neighbours, or has been responsible for any act of harassment on the grounds of race, colour, religion, sex, sexual orientation, or disability, or has been convicted of using the property for immoral or illegal purposes; (Ground 14) or because of domestic violence (Ground 14A)
Where the tenancy has devolved under the will or intestacy of the Tenant
Suitable alternative accommodation is available to the Tenant

Notice Periods for ending Assured Tenancy- 4.3-Before the expiry of the fixed term the landlord agrees that it will not give less than four weeks notice in writing of its intention to seek a possession order except where it is seeking possession on Ground 14 or Ground 14A (whether or not combined with other Grounds) where it shall give such period of notice that it shall decide and that is not less than the statutory minimum notice period

144

Expiry of Tenancy- 4.4-The landlord can only end the Tenancy by giving the Tenant at least two months notice that it requires possession of the Premises and by obtaining a court order for possession. The court will make an order for possession if it is satisfied that the proper notice has been given.

Cessation of Assured Tenancy- 4.5-If the Tenancy ceases to be an assured tenancy the landlord may end the Tenancy by giving four weeks' notice in writing which shall be validly served on the Tenant if posted or delivered to the Premises.

****

**Department for
Communities and
Local Government**

FORM 6A
Notice seeking possession of a property let on an Assured Shorthold Tenancy

Housing Act 1988 section 21(1) and (4) as amended by section 194 and paragraph 103 of Schedule 11 to the Local Government and Housing Act 1989 and section 98(2) and (3) of the Housing Act 1996

Please write clearly in black ink. Please tick boxes where appropriate.

This form should be used where a no fault possession of accommodation let under an assured shorthold tenancy (AST) is sought under section 21(1) or (4) of the Housing Act 1988.

There are certain circumstances in which the law says that you cannot seek possession against your tenant using section 21 of the Housing Act 1988, in which case you should not use this form. These are:

    (a) during the first four months of the tenancy (but where the tenancy is a replacement tenancy, the four month period is calculated by reference to the start of the original tenancy and not the start of the replacement tenancy – see section 21(4B) of the Housing Act 1988);

    (b) where the landlord is prevented from retaliatory eviction under section 33 of the Deregulation Act 2015;

    (c) where the landlord has not provided the tenant with an energy performance certificate, gas safety certificate or the Department for Communities and Local Government's publication "How to rent: the checklist for renting in England" (see the Assured Shorthold Tenancy Notices and Prescribed Requirements (England) Regulations 2015);

    (d) where the landlord has not complied with the tenancy deposit protection legislation; or

    (e) where a property requires a licence but is unlicensed.

    Landlords who are unsure about whether they are affected by these provisions should seek specialist advice.

This form must be used for all ASTs created on or after 1 October 2015 except for statutory periodic tenancies which have come into being on or after 1 October 2015 at the end of fixed term ASTs created before 1 October 2015. There is no obligation to use this form in relation to ASTs created prior to 1 October 2015, however it may nevertheless be used for all ASTs.

at to do if this notice is served on you

should read this notice very carefully. It explains that your landlord has started the process to regain session of the property referred to in section 2 below.

are entitled to at least two months' notice before being required to give up possession of the property. vever, if your tenancy started on a periodic basis without any initial fixed term a longer notice period may equired depending on how often you are required to pay rent (for example, if you pay rent quarterly, you st be given at least three months' notice, or, if you have a periodic tenancy which is half yearly or annual, must be given at least six months' notice (which is the maximum)). The date you are required to leave uld be shown in section 2 below. After this date the landlord can apply to court for a possession order inst you.

ere your tenancy is terminated before the end of a period of your tenancy (e.g. where you pay rent in ance on the first of each month and you are required to give up possession in the middle of the month), may be entitled to repayment of rent from the landlord under section 21C of the Housing Act 1988.

u need advice about this notice, and what you should do about it, take it immediately to a citizens' advice eau, a housing advice centre, a law centre or a solicitor.

To:

Name(s) of tenant(s) (Block Capitals)

You are required to leave the below address after [   ] [1]. If you do not leave, your landlord may apply to the court for an order under section 21(1) or (4) of the Housing Act 1988 requiring you to give up possession.

Address of premises

---

andlords should insert a calendar date here. The date should allow sufficient time to ensure that the notice is properly served on the enant(s). This will depend on the method of service being used and landlords should check whether the tenancy agreement makes specific rovision about service. Where landlords are seeking an order for possession on a periodic tenancy under section 21(4) of the Housing Act 988, the notice period should also not be shorter than the period of the tenancy (up to a maximum of six months), e.g. where there is a uarterly periodic tenancy, the date should be three months from the date of service.

Form 6A

3. This notice is valid for six months only from the date of issue unless you have a periodic tenancy under which more than two months' notice is required (see notes accompanying this form) in which case the notice is valid for four months only from the date specified in section 2 above.

4. Name and address of landlord

To be signed and dated by the landlord or their agent (someone acting for them). If there are joint landlords each landlord or the agent should sign unless one signs on behalf of the rest with their agreement.

Signed   Date (DD/MM/YYYY)

Please specify whether: ☐ landlord   ☐ joint landlords   ☐ landlord's agent

Name(s) of signatory/signatories (Block Capitals)

Address(es) of signatory/signatories

Telephone of signatory/signatories

3

**Department for
Communities and
Local Government**

Notice seeking possession of a property let on an Assured Shorthold Tenancy (Form 6a)

This form should be used where a no fault possession of accommodation let under an assured shorthold tenancy (AST) is sought under section 21(1) or (4) of the Housing Act 1988.

This form must be used for all ASTs created on or after 1 October 2015 except for statutory periodic tenancies which have come into being on or after 1 October 2015 at the end of fixed term ASTs created before 1 October 2015.

The validity period of this form is six months following the date of its issue unless the tenancy is a periodic tenancy under which more than two months' notice is required, in which case the validity period is four months from the date the tenant is required to leave (see notes accompanying the form).

You cannot use this form:

> in the first four months of the tenancy (but where the tenancy is a replacement tenancy, the four month period is calculated by reference to the start of the original tenancy and not the start of the replacement tenancy – see section 21(4B) of the Housing Act 1988);
>
> where the landlord is prevented from retaliatory eviction under section 33 of the Deregulation Act 2015;
>
> where the landlord has not provided the prescribed information and/or prescribed documents as set out below;
>
> where the landlord has not complied with the tenancy deposit protection legislation; or
>
> where a property requires a licence but is unlicensed.

Prescribed Information

The landlord is required to provide a copy of the Department for Communities and Local Government's publication "How to rent: the checklist for renting in England" by providing a pdf copy (which may be obtained from www.gov.uk/government/publications/how-to-rent). We recommend that this should be given at the start of the tenancy. Landlords are not required to supply a further copy of the publication each time a different version is published during the tenancy.

Where the landlord has failed to provide the publication, this form may not be used. However, this restriction is lifted as soon as the publication has been provided.

The requirement does not apply where a landlord is a private registered provider of social housing or where a landlord has already provided the tenant with an up-to-date version of the booklet under an earlier tenancy.

If the tenant has not notified the landlord, or a person acting on behalf of the landlord, of an e-mail address at which the tenant is content to accept service of notices and other documents given under or in connection with the tenancy, the landlord must provide a paper copy of the publication.

Prescribed documents:

Where the landlord has failed to comply with certain existing legal obligations, this form may not be used. However, this restriction is lifted as soon as the obligations have been complied with. The obligations are the requirement on a landlord to provide the tenant with:

- an Energy Performance Certificate (Reg 6(5), The Energy Performance of Buildings (England and Wales) Regulations 2012); and

- a gas safety certificate (Reg 36(6)(a), The Gas Safety (Installation and Use) Regulations 1998)

Tenants that need advice about this notice, and what to do about it, should take it immediately to a citizens' advice bureau, a housing advice centre, a law centre or a solicitor.

Tenants can also get expert, independent advice free from Shelterline on 0808 800 4444. Their advisers will be able to give expert advice, independent advice.

SHORT ASSURED TENANCY AGREEMENT

This is a Short Assured Tenancy within the meaning of section 32 of the Housing (Scotland) Act 1988

1. **PARTIES**

    THE LANDLORD IS:_____
    ("The Landlord")

    LANDLORD ADDRESS:_____

    _____

    _____

    LANDLORD TEL. NO:_____

    HMO 24 HOUR CONTACT NO. _____

    LANDLORD REGISTRATION NO. _ _ _ _ _ _ _ / _ _ _ / _ _ _ _ _

    THE TENANT IS/ARE:_____

    _____

    _____

    _____

    _____

    ("The Tenant (s)")

    Where this is a joint tenancy, the term "Tenant" applies to each of the individuals above and the full responsibilities and rights set out in this Agreement apply to each Tenant who will be jointly and severally liable.

2. **SUBJECTS**

    THE ACCOMMODATION LET IS:_____

    _____

    _____

    _____

    ("The Property address or identified room")

3. **COMMENCEMENT & DURATION:**

The tenancy will commence on _____ ("The start Date")

and will end on: _____ ("The end Date").

If the agreement is not brought to an end by either party on the end date, it will continue thereafter on a monthly basis until ended by either party.

4. **RENT AND OTHER CHARGES**

4.1 The rent is £_____ per calendar month payable monthly (in advance). The first payment will be paid at date of entry or before and subsequent payments are due and must be paid on or before the same date of each calendar month thereafter.

4.2 The Landlord may propose to increase the rent after the end date specified at Clause 3 above. Under such circumstances the Tenant will be given a minimum of 1 month's notice in writing of any proposed change before the beginning of the rental period when the change is to start.

5 **SERVICES**

The following services will be provided

(list the services together with the prices).

The Tenant hereby agrees to pay the service charges as required.

6 **DEPOSIT**

At the date of entry or before, a deposit of £ _____ will be paid by the Tenant to the Landlord or his agents. The Landlord or his agent will issue a receipt for the deposit to the Tenant. No interest shall be paid by the Landlord to the Tenant for the deposit.

6.1 The deposit will be paid into a tenancy deposit scheme within the timescales laid out in the **Tenancy Deposit Schemes (Scotland) Regulations 2011.**

6.2 The scheme administrator is _____

6.3 The Landlord will be entitled at the expiry or end of the lease to use the deposit to meet any outstanding sums or accounts due by the Tenant, the cost of repairing or replacing any of the fittings and fixtures which have been broken, damaged or lost and the expense of making good any failure by the Tenant to fulfil any of the other conditions of this lease.

6.4 The deposit or part of the deposit, if any, will be refunded to the Tenant within the timescales as laid out in the **Tenancy Deposit Schemes (Scotland) Regulations 2011**

7 CONTENTS

The Tenant agrees that the signed Inventory, attached as Schedule 1 to this Agreement is a full and accurate record of the contents of the accommodation at the start of the tenancy. The Tenant has a period of seven days after signing the Inventory to ensure that the Inventory is correct and to tell the Landlord of any discrepancies in writing, after which the Tenant shall be deemed to be fully satisfied with the terms.

7.1 The Tenant agrees that these contents were as described in the inventory. The Tenant agrees to replace or repair (or to pay the cost, at the option of the Landlord) any of the contents which are destroyed, damaged, removed or lost during the tenancy, fair wear and tear excepted. The costs involved in making good any damage or cleaning found necessary may be deducted by the Landlord from the deposit under Clause **6**

8 LOCAL AUTHORITY TAXES

The Tenant will be responsible for payment of the council tax and water and sewerage charges, or any local tax which may replace this. The Tenant will advise the local authority of the date of the start of the tenancy and the date of the end of the tenancy.

9 HOUSEHOLD BILLS

The Tenant undertakes to ensure that the accounts for the supply to the accommodation of gas, electricity and telephone are entered in his name with the relevant supplier. The Tenant agrees to pay promptly all sums that become due for these supplies relative to the period of the tenancy.

9.1 The Tenant agrees to make the necessary arrangements with the suppliers to settle all accounts for these services on termination of the tenancy. The Tenant agrees not to change supplier without the prior written permission of the Landlord. The Landlord may keep from the deposit any sum the Landlord expends or incurs in settling final accounts for the services at the end of the tenancy.

10 INSURANCE

The Landlord undertakes to pay all premiums for insurance of the building and contents belonging to him. The Landlord will have no liability for any items belonging to the Tenant. The Tenant is responsible for arranging insurance of his own belongings.

11 OCCUPATION AND USE OF THE ACCOMMODATION

11.1 ONLY OR PRINCIPAL HOME

The Tenant agrees to occupy the accommodation as his only or principal home and not to carry on any formal or registered trade business or profession there.

11.2 ABSENCES

The Tenant agrees to tell the Landlord if he is to be absent from the accommodation for any reason for a period of more than fourteen days. The Tenant agrees to take such measures to secure the accommodation prior to such absence as the Landlord may reasonably require and take appropriate measures to prevent frost or flood damage.

11.3 SUBLETTING & LODGERS

The Tenant agrees not to:
i. assign this tenancy to any other person; or
ii. sublet the accommodation in whole or in part; or
iii. take in lodgers or paying guests; or
iv. allow other persons to share the occupation of the premises, whether or not for payment, without the prior written consent of the Landlord.

11.4 REASONABLE CARE

The Tenant agrees to take reasonable care of the accommodation and any common parts, and in particular agrees to take all reasonable steps to:
i. keep the accommodation adequately ventilated and heated;
ii. not bring any hazardous or combustible goods or material into the accommodation;
iii. not pour any oil, grease, or other damaging materials down the drains or waste pipes;
iv. prevent water pipes freezing in cold weather;
v. avoid danger to the accommodation or neighbouring properties by way of fire or flooding;
vi. ensure the property and its fixtures and fittings are kept clean during the tenancy;
vii. not Interfere with the smoke detectors, heat detectors or the fire alarm system;
viii. not Interfere with door closer mechanisms.

11.5 ALTERATIONS

The Tenant agrees not to make any alteration to the accommodation, its fixtures or fittings, nor to carry out any internal or external decoration without the prior written consent of the Landlord.

Any request for adaptations, auxiliary aids or services as per the Equalities Act 2010 or the Housing (Scotland) Act 2006 must be made in writing to the Landlord. Consent for alterations requested under this legislation will not reasonably be withheld.

11.6 COMMON PARTS

In the case of flatted property the Tenant agrees, in conjunction with the other proprietors / occupiers, to sweep and clean the common stairway and to co-operate with other proprietors/properties in keeping the garden, back green or other communal areas clean and tidy.

Where a tenant fails in this responsibility, the Landlord may carry out these responsibilities and recover the costs from the Tenant.

11.7 ROOF

The Tenant is not permitted to access the roof.

11.8 REFUSE

The Tenant agrees to dispose of all rubbish in an appropriate manner and at the appropriate time. Rubbish must not be placed anywhere in the common stair at any time. The Tenant must take reasonable care to ensure that the rubbish is properly bagged. If rubbish is normally collected from the street it should not be put out earlier than 7am on the day of collection. Rubbish containers should be returned to their normal storage places as soon as possible after the rubbish has been collected. The Tenant must comply with any local arrangements for the disposal of large items (such as large electrical items).

11.9 STORAGE

Nothing belonging to the Tenant or anyone living with the Tenant or the visitors may be left or stored in the common stair if it causes nuisance or annoyance to neighbours.

11.10 DANGEROUS SUBSTANCES

The Tenant must not store keep on or bring into the premises or any store, shed or garage, inflammable liquids or explosive gasses which might reasonably be considered to be a fire hazard or otherwise dangerous to the premises or its occupants or the neighbours or the neighbour's property.

12   **RESPECT FOR OTHERS**

12.1   The Tenant, those living with him/her, and his/her visitors must not harass or act in an antisocial manner to, or pursue a course of antisocial conduct against any person in the neighbourhood. Such people include residents, visitors, agents and contractors and those in the Tenant's house.

12.2   "Antisocial" means causing or likely to cause alarm, distress, nuisance or annoyance to any person or causing damage to anyone's property. Harassment of a person includes causing the person alarm or distress. Antisocial conduct includes speech.
A course of conduct means antisocial behaviour on at least two occasions.

12.3   In particular, the Tenant, those living with him/her, and his/her visitors must not:

     i.   make excessive noise. This includes, but is not limited to, the use of televisions, hi-fis, radios and musical instruments and DIY tools;

     ii.   fail to control pets properly or allow them to foul or cause damage to other people's property;

     iii.   allow visitors to the Tenant's house to be noisy or disruptive;

     iv.   use the Tenant's house or allow it to be used, for illegal or immoral purposes;

v. vandalise or damage the Landlord's property or any part of the common parts or neighbourhood;

vi. leave rubbish ether in unauthorised places or at inappropriate times;

vii. allow his/her children to cause nuisance or annoyance to other people by failing to exercise reasonable control over them;

viii. harass, threaten or assault any other Tenant, member of his/her household, visitors, neighbours, members or employees of the Landlord or any other person or persons in the house, or neighbourhood, for whatever reason. This includes behaviour due to that person's race colour or ethnic origin, nationality, gender, sexuality, disability, age, religion or other belief, or other status;

ix. use or carry offensive weapons;

x. use or sell unlawful drugs or sell alcohol;

xi. store or bring onto the premises any type of firearm or firearm ammunition including any replica or decommissioned firearms.

The particular prohibitions on behaviour listed above do not in any way restrict the general responsibilities of the Tenant .

13. PETS

The Tenant agrees not to keep any animals or pets In the accommodation without the prior written consent of the Landlord. Any such consent will not be unreasonably withheld. Any pet (where permitted) will be kept under supervision and control to ensure that it does not cause deterioration in the accommodation, deterioration in the condition of common areas, nuisance either to neighbours or in the locality of the property.

14. ACCESS

14.1 ROUTINE ACCESS

The Tenant agrees to give the Landlord access to the accommodation for the purpose of carrying out maintenance, repair or inspection, providing that written notice has been given to the Tenant no later than 24 hours beforehand that such access is required.

14.2 EMERGENCY ACCESS

The Tenant agrees to give immediate access to the Landlord in an emergency whether or not notice has been given. The Landlord reserves the right to effect forcible entry to the accommodation should such access not be made available.

14.3 KEYS

The tenant has been given a key agreement that sets out the circumstances for the retention and use of keys by the landlord.

15 REPAIRS AND MAINTENANCE

15.1 THE REPAIRING STANDARD

The Landlord must ensure that the accommodation meets the Repairing Standard at the start of the tenancy and at all times during the tenancy. During the tenancy this duty applies only when the Tenant informs the

Landlord of work required or the Landlord becomes aware of it in some other way (inspection visit).

The Repairing Standard does not cover work for which you, as the Tenant, are responsible due to your duty to use the house in a proper manner; nor does it cover the repair or maintenance of anything that you are entitled to remove from the house.

If you believe that the landlord has failed to ensure that the house meets the Repairing Standard at all times during the tenancy, you have the right to apply to the Private Rented Housing Panel (PRHP). The PRHP may reject the application; consider whether the case can be resolved by us (the Tenant and Landlord) ourselves (for example, by agreeing to mediation); or refer your application to a Private Rented Housing Committee (PRHC) for consideration. The PRHC has power to require a Landlord to carry out work necessary to meet the Repairing Standard.

15.2 HABITABILITY

The Landlord agrees throughout the period of the tenancy to maintain the accommodation in a wind and watertight condition and in all other respects reasonably fit for human habitation.

15.3 STRUCTURE & EXTERIOR

The Landlord undertakes (together with any other owners of common parts of the building in which the accommodation is situated, if appropriate) to keep in repair the structure and exterior of the accommodation including the following:

i.   drains, gutters and external pipes;
ii.   roof;
iii.   outside walls, doors, windowsills, window catches, sash cords, and window frames;
iv.   internal walls, floors, ceilings, doors, door frames, internal stair cases and landings;
v.   chimneys, chimney stacks, and flues (including sweeping);
vi.   pathways, steps or other means of access;
vii.   plaster work;
viii   boundary walls and fences.

15.4 GAS SAFETY

The Landlord must ensure that there is an annual Gas safety check on all pipework and appliances. The check must be carried out by a Gas Safe Registered installer. The Tenant must be given a copy of the Landlords gas safety certificate. The Landlord must keep certificates for at least two years. The Gas Safety (Installation and use) Regulations 1998 places duties on Tenants to report any defects with gas pipework or gas appliances that they are aware of to the Landlord or letting agent. Tenants are forbidden to use appliances that have been deemed unsafe by a gas contractor.

15.5 LIQUID PETROLEUM GAS (LPG)

The use or storage of LPG is not permitted in the property.

15.6 INSTALLATIONS

The Landlord will keep in repair and in proper working order the installations in the accommodation for the supply of water, gas, electricity, sanitation, space heating and water heating (with the exception of those installed by the Tenant or which the Tenant is entitled to remove) including the following:

i.   basins, sinks, baths, toilets, and showers;

ii. gas or electric fires and central heating systems;

iii. electrical wiring;

iv. door entry systems;

v.   cookers;

vi. extractor fans.

vii smoke alarms

15.7 DEFECTIVE FIXTURES AND FITTINGS

The Landlord will repair or replace any of the fixtures, fittings or furnishings, supplied by the Landlord in the accommodation, which become defective through usual wear and tear; and will do so within a reasonable period of time. Nothing contained in this Agreement makes the Landlord responsible for repairing damage caused wilfully or negligently by the Tenant, anyone living with the Tenant or an invited visitor to the property. Should the Landlord be required to carry out the work, the Tenant must pay the cost of the repair. The Tenant hereby agrees to pay the costs of repair. This paragraph does not apply to damage caused by fair, wear and tear or vandals (provided that the Tenant has reported the damage to the Police and to the Landlord as soon as the damage is discovered).

15.8 REPAIR TIMETABLE

The Tenant undertakes to immediately notify the Landlord (or any officer, agent or employee specified by the Landlord for that purpose) of the need for any repair or emergency. The Landlord undertakes to carry out necessary repairs within a reasonable period of time after having been notified of the need to do so.

15.9 PAYMENT FOR REPAIRS

The Tenant will be liable for the cost of repairs where the need for them is attributable to his fault or negligence, that of any person residing with him, or any guest of his. The Landlord may deduct such costs at the termination of the tenancy from the deposit under Clause **6**.

16. LEGISLATION

The Landlord undertakes to secure repossession only by lawful means and to comply with all relevant legislation affecting private sector residential tenancies, and, where applicable, all legislation relating to other activities carried on in the premises, such as the provision of care or support, or food preparation.

17. DATA PROTECTION

Landlords and letting agents may share details about the performance of obligations under this agreement by the Landlord and Tenant; past, present and future known addresses of the parties, with each other, with credit and reference providers for referencing purposes and rental decisions; with Utility and Water Companies, local authority Council Tax and Housing Benefit departments, Mortgage lenders, to help prevent dishonesty, for administrative and accounting purposes, or for occasional debt tracing and fraud prevention. Under the Data Protection Act 1998 you are entitled, on payment of a fee which will be no greater than that set by statute, to see a copy of personal information held about you and to have it amended if it is shown to be incorrect.

18. ENDING THE TENANCY

This Short Assured Tenancy may be ended by:-

18.1 The tenancy reaching its end date and the Landlord giving two month's prior written notice that possession of the house is required in terms of section 33 of the Housing (Scotland) Act 1988 at that end date.

18.2 By the Landlord serving on the Tenant a Notice to Quit. The Landlord may serve such notice either:

   i. To terminate the tenancy at its end date

   ii. To terminate the tenancy where the Tenant has broken or not performed any of the obligations under this agreement.

18.3 By the Tenant giving the Landlord one month's notice in writing to terminate the tenancy at its termination date.

18.4 By the Landlord giving the Tenant the required Notice in the prescribed format in terms of Section 19 of the Housing (Scotland) Act 1988 of their intention to commence proceedings and then subsequently obtaining an order for recovery of possession from the Sheriff Court on one or more of the following grounds set out in schedule 5 of the Housing (Scotland) Act 1988. These grounds are as follows:-

HOUSING (SCOTLAND) ACT 1988: SECTION 18 (6) AND SCHEDULE 5 PARTS I AND II

Grounds 1-8 set out in Part 1 below are mandatory grounds: that is, if they are established the Sheriff must grant an order for possession.

Grounds 9-17 set out in Part II below are discretionary grounds: that is, even if they are established, the Sheriff will grant an order for possession only if he believes it is reasonable to do so.

Ground 1

Not later than the beginning of the tenancy the Landlord (or, where there are joint Landlords, any of them) gave notice in writing to the Tenant that possession might be recovered on this Ground or the sheriff is of the opinion that it is reasonable to dispense with the requirement of notice and (in either case)-

(a) at any time before the beginning of the tenancy, the Landlord who is seeking possession or, in the case of joint Landlords seeking possession, at least one of them occupied the house as his only or principal home; or

(b) the Landlord who is seeking possession or, in the case of joint Landlords seeking possession, at least one of them requires the house as his or his spouse's only or principal home, and neither the Landlord (or, in the case of joint Landlords, any one of them) nor any other person who, as Landlord, derived title from the Landlord who gave the notice mentioned above acquired the Landlord's interest in the tenancy for value.

Ground 2

The house is subject to a heritable security granted before the creation of the tenancy and-

(a) as a result of a default by the debtor the creditor is entitled to sell the house and requires it for the purpose of disposing of it with vacant possession in exercise of that entitlement; and

(b) either notice was given in writing to the Tenant not later than the date of commencement of the tenancy that possession might be recovered on this Ground or the Sheriff is satisfied that it is reasonable to dispense with the requirement of notice.

Ground 3

The house is let under a tenancy for a specified period not exceeding eight months and-

(a) not later than the date of commencement of the tenancy the Landlord (or, where there are joint Landlords, any of them) gave notice in writing to the Tenant that possession might be recovered under this Ground; and

(b) the house was, at some time within the period of 12 months ending on that date, occupied under a right to occupy it for a holiday; and for the purposes of this Ground a tenancy shall be treated as being for a specified period-

(I) not exceeding eight months, if it is determinable at the option of the Landlord (other than in the event of an irritancy being incurred) before the expiration of eight months from the commencement of the period of the tenancy; and

(ii) exceeding eight months, if it confers on the Tenant an option for renewal of the tenancy for a period which, together with the original period, exceeds eight months, and it is not determinable as mentioned in paragraph (i) above.

Ground 4

Where the house is let under a tenancy for a specified period not exceeding 12 months and-

(a) not later than the date of commencement of the tenancy the Landlord (or, where there are joint Landlords, any of them) gave notice in writing to the Tenant that possession might be recovered on this Ground; and (b)　at some time within the period of 12 months ending on that date the house was subject to such a tenancy as is referred to in paragraph 7(1) of Schedule 4 to this Act; and for the purposes of this Ground a tenancy shall be treated as being for a specified period-

(i)　not exceeding 12 months, if it is determinable at the option of the Landlord (other than in the event of an irritancy being incurred) before the expiration of 12 months from the commencement of the period of the tenancy; and

(ii)　exceeding 12 months, if it confers on the Tenant an option for renewal of the tenancy for a period which, together with the original period, exceeds 12 months, and it is not determinable as mentioned in paragraph (i) above.

Ground 5

The house is held for the purpose of being available for occupation by a minister or a full-time lay missionary of any religious denomination as a residence from which to perform the duties of his office and-

(a)　not later than the beginning of the tenancy the Landlord (or, where there are joint Landlords, any of them) gave notice in writing to the Tenant that possession might be recovered on this ground; and

(b)　the sheriff is satisfied that the house is required for occupation by such a minister or missionary as such a residence.

Ground 6

The Landlord who is seeking possession or, where the immediate Landlord is a registered housing association within the meaning of the [1985 c. 69.] Housing Associations Act 1985, a superior Landlord intends to demolish or reconstruct the whole or a substantial part of the house or to carry out substantial works on the house or any part thereof or any building of which it forms part and the following conditions are fulfilled (and in those conditions the Landlord who is intending to carry out the demolition, reconstruction or substantial works is referred to as "the relevant Landlord")—

(a)　either-

(i)　the relevant Landlord (or, in the case of joint relevant Landlords, any one of them) acquired his interest in the house before the creation of the tenancy; or

(ii)　none of the following persons acquired his interest in the house for value—

(A)　the relevant Landlord (or, in the case of joint relevant Landlords, any one of them);

(B)　the immediate Landlord (or, in the case of joint immediate Landlords, any one of them), where he acquired his interest after the creation of the tenancy;

(C)　any person from whom the relevant Landlord (or any one of joint relevant Landlords) derives title and who acquired his interest in the house after the creation of the tenancy; and

(b)　the relevant Landlord cannot reasonably carry out the intended work without the Tenant giving up possession of the house because-

(i)   the work can otherwise be carried out only if the Tenant accepts a variation in the terms of the tenancy and the Tenant refuses to do so;

(ii)   the work can otherwise be carried out only if the Tenant accepts an assured tenancy of part of the house and the Tenant refuses to do so; or

(iii) the work can otherwise be carried out only if the Tenant accepts either a variation in the terms of the tenancy or an assured tenancy of part of the house or both, and the Tenant refuses to do so; or

(iv) the work cannot otherwise be carried out even if the Tenant accepts a variation in the terms of the tenancy or an assured tenancy of only part of the house or both.

Ground 7

The tenancy has devolved under the will or intestacy of the former Tenant and the proceedings for the recovery of possession are begun not later than twelve months after the death of the former Tenant or, if the sheriff so directs, after the date on which, in his opinion, the Landlord (or, where there are joint Landlords, any of them) became aware of the former Tenant's death. For the purposes of this Ground, the acceptance by the Landlord of rent from a new Tenant after the death of the former Tenant shall not be regarded as creating a new tenancy, unless the Landlord agrees in writing to a change (as compared with the tenancy before the death) in the amount of the rent, the period of the tenancy, the premises which are let or any other term of the tenancy.

Ground 8

Both at the date of the service of the notice under section 19 of this Act relating to the proceedings for possession and at the date of the hearing, at least three months rent lawfully due from the Tenant is in arrears.

Ground 9

Suitable alternative accommodation is available for the Tenant or will be available for him when the order for possession takes effect.

Ground 10

The following conditions are fulfilled-

(a) the Tenant has given a notice to quit which has expired; and

(b) the Tenant has remained in possession of the whole or any part of the house; and

(c) proceedings for the recovery of possession have been begun not more than six months after the expiry of the notice to quit; and

(d) the Tenant is not entitled to possession of the house by virtue of a new tenancy.

Ground 11

Whether or not any rent is in arrears on the date on which proceedings for possession are begun, the Tenant has persistently delayed paying rent, which has become lawfully due.

Ground 12

Some rent lawfully due from the Tenant-
- (a) is unpaid on the date on which the proceedings for possession are begun; and
- (b) except where subsection (1)(b) of section 19 of this Act applies, was in arrears at the date of the service of the notice under that section relating to those proceedings.

Ground 13

Any obligation of the tenancy (other than one related to the payment of rent) has been broken or not performed.

Ground 14

The condition of the house or of any of the common parts has deteriorated owing to acts of waste by, or the neglect or default of, the Tenant or any one of joint Tenants or any person residing or lodging with him or any sub-tenant of his; and, in the case of acts of waste by, or the neglect or default of, a person lodging with a Tenant or a sub-tenant of his, the Tenant has not, before the making of the order in question, taken such steps as he ought reasonably to have taken for the removal of the lodger or sub-tenant. In this Ground, "the common parts" means any part of a building containing the house and any other premises, which the Tenant is entitled under the terms of the tenancy to use in common with the occupiers of other houses.

Ground 15

The Tenant, a person residing or lodging in the house with the Tenant or a person visiting the house has-
- (a) been convicted of-
  - (i) using or allowing the house to be used for immoral or illegal purposes; or
  - (ii) an offence punishable by imprisonment committed in, or in the locality of, the house; or
- (b) acted in an antisocial manner in relation to a person residing, visiting or otherwise engaging in lawful activity in the locality; or
- (c) pursued a course of antisocial conduct in relation to such a person as is mentioned in head (b) above.

In this Ground "antisocial", in relation to an action or course of conduct, means causing or likely to cause alarm, distress, nuisance or annoyance, "conduct" includes speech and a course of conduct must involve conduct on at least two occasions and "Tenant" includes any one of joint Tenants."

Ground 16

The condition of any furniture provided for use under the tenancy has deteriorated owing to ill-treatment by the Tenant or any other person residing or lodging with him in the house and, in the case of ill-treatment by a person lodging with the Tenant or by a sub-tenant of his, the Tenant has not taken such steps as he ought reasonably to have taken for the removal of the lodger or sub-tenant.

Ground 17

The house was let to the Tenant in consequence of his employment by the Landlord seeking possession or a previous Landlord under the tenancy and the Tenant has ceased to be in that employment.

19. NOTICE & DECLARATIONS

In signing this Agreement and taking entry to the accommodation, the Tenant:

i. acknowledges that he was served a Form AT5, before the creation of this tenancy, and that he understands this tenancy to be a Short Assured Tenancy within the meaning of section 32 of the Housing (Scotland) Act 1988;

ii. confirms that he has made full and true disclosure of all information sought by the Landlord in connection with the granting of this tenancy

iii. confirms that he has not knowingly or carelessly made any false or misleading statements (whether written or oral) which might affect the Landlord's decision to grant the tenancy.

20. INTERPRETATION

Declaring for the purposes of this lease that words importing the masculine gender shall include the feminine; words importing the singular shall include the plural, and where there are two or more persons included in the expression "the Tenant" the obligations and conditions incumbent upon and expressed to be made by "the Tenant", including payment of the rent, shall be held to bind all such persons jointly and severally.

Tenant Signature 1		Witness Signature	
Tenant Full Name (Block Capitals)		Witness Full Name (Block Capitals)	
Tenant Address		Witness Address	
Date:	Time:	Date:	Time:

Tenant Signature 2		Witness Signature	
Tenant Full Name (Block Capitals)		Witness Full Name (Block Capitals)	
Tenant Address		Witness Address	
Date:	Time:	Date:	Time:

Tenant Signature 3	Witness Signature
Tenant Full Name (Block Capitals)	Witness Full Name (Block Capitals)
Tenant Address	Witness Address
Date: Time:	Date: Time:
Tenant Signature 4	Witness Signature
Tenant Full Name (Block Capitals)	Witness Full Name (Block Capitals)
Tenant Address	Witness Address
Date: Time:	Date: Time:
Tenant Signature 5	Witness Signature
Tenant Full Name (Block Capitals)	Witness Full Name (Block Capitals)
Tenant Address	Witness Address
Date: Time:	Date: Time:
Landlord Signature	Witness Signature
Landlord Full Name (Block Capitals)	Witness Full Name (Block Capitals)
Landlord Address	Witness Address
Date: Time:	Date: Time:

LANDLORDS NOTICE TO TERMINATE
SHORT ASSURED TENANCY

FROM:

LANDLORDS NAME AND
ADDRESS_____

_____

_____

_____

TO:
TENANT_____

_____

_____

_____

DATE_____

PROPERTY_____

_____

_____

_____

The above landlord hereby gives formal notice to the above tenant under section 33 of the Housing (Scotland) Act 1988 of their intention to bring the tenants tenancy to an end and recover possession of the above property currently occupied by the tenant.

In terms of section 33 of the aforementioned Act the tenant must receive at least two months notice of the landlords intention to recover possession. Please therefore take note that you are required to vacate the premises no later than_____

Note: This Notice to terminate and the Notice to Quit overleaf should both be completed and sent to the tenant at least two months before the end of the tenancy.

SCOTLAND

SHORT ASSURED TENANCY NOTICE TO QUIT

NOTICE OF REMOVAL UNDER SECTION 37 OF THE
SHERIFF COURTS (SCOTLAND) ACT 1907

FROM:
LANDLORD_____
_____
_____

TO:
TENANT_____
_____
_____

DATE:_____

PROPERTY_____
_____

The above landlords hereby give notice to the above tenant that the
tenant is required to remove from the property at the_____ day
of_____ in terms of the lease between landlord and tenant.

The undernoted schedule which is incorporated herein complied
with the Assured Tenancies (Notice to Quit Information) (Scotland)
Regulations 1988.

Schedule

1. Even after the Notice to Quit has run out, before the tenant can be lawfully evicted, the landlord must get an order or possession from the court.

2. If the landlord issues a Notice to Quit but does not seek to gain possession of the property in question the contractual assured tenancy which has been terminated will be replaced by a Statutory Assured Tenancy. In such circumstances the landlord may propose new terms for the tenancy and may seek an adjustment to the rent at annual intervals thereafter.

3. If a tenant does not know what type of tenancy he has or is otherwise unsure of his rights he can obtain advice from a solicitor. Help with all or part of the cost of legal advice and assistance can be available under the legal aid legislation. A tenant can also seek help from a Citizens Advice Bureau or Housing Advisory centre.

Sample Lodger Agreement

This is an example of a Lodger agreement between the owner of a property, referred to as The Landlord and a Lodger.

1. Parties

The Landlord's full name: _____

Landlord's address: _____

_____

Landlord's tel. no: _____

The Lodger's full name: _____

2. Accommodation

Shared areas: (Details of the areas of the property shared with the landlord, e.g. lounge, bathroom, kitchen, hallway etc)

Lodger's accommodation: (Details of the room(s) that the Lodger has exclusive possession of, e.g. a bedroom, a cupboard etc)

3. Start date and duration

The occupancy agreement will start on: __ / __ / ____ ("The start date")

The occupancy agreement will end on: __ / __ / ____ ("The end date")

4. Rent

The rent is £ _____ per calendar month paid monthly/weekly in advance. The first payment will be paid on the start date and the subsequent payments will be paid on the same date of each calendar month/same day each week thereafter. Should the Lodger fail to pay the rent the Landlord may serve upon them a notice for payment/removal or apply to court for payment/removal.

5. Council tax and utilities (Where council tax and utilities are not included in the monthly rent then details of the frequency and likely costs should be stated here)

Council tax and utilities are included in the monthly rent/The Lodger is responsible for paying their share of the council tax and utility bills. (Delete as appropriate or specify the type, frequency and total cost) Should the Lodger fail to pay their share of the council tax and/or utility bills the Landlord may serve upon them a notice for payment/removal and/or apply to court for removal/payment.

6. Deposit

On or before the start date a deposit of £ _____ will be paid by the Lodger to the Landlord. The Landlord will give the Lodger a receipt for the deposit.

The Landlord will be entitled at the end of the occupancy agreement to deduct from the deposit any sums due by the Lodger to cover the cost of repairing or replacing any broken, damaged or lost items and the expense of making good any failure by the Lodger to fulfil any other conditions of the occupancy agreement.

The deposit or remainder of the deposit will be refunded to the Lodger within 14 days, or as soon as possible after the termination of the occupancy agreement. A list of deductions from the deposit will be attached where deductions have been made, notwithstanding fair wear and tear. Where deductions have been made from the deposit copies of receipts for any money deducted will be sent to the Lodger.

7. Contents

The Lodger agrees that the signed inventory is complete and accurate at the beginning of the Lodger agreement. The Lodger has a period of 7 days within which to make sure that the inventory is accurate and inform the landlord of any mistakes. The landlord has the right to deduct from the deposit any costs incurred from the damage or destruction of any items on the inventory caused by the Lodger.

8. Insurance

It is the Lodger's responsibility to insure their personal affects.

9. Duty to take reasonable care of the property

The Lodger agrees to take reasonable care of the property and the common areas by keeping their room clean and tidy and taking reasonable steps to avoid causing damage to the property. The Lodger accepts liability for any damage caused to the Landlord's property by them and will bear the costs of any repairs necessary as a result of such damage.

10. Respect for others

The Lodger must not: act in an antisocial manner towards the Landlord or any visitor to the property; make excessive noise; allow any visitors to act in an antisocial manner; leave rubbish in inappropriate places; use the property for illegal purposes.

11. Pets

The Lodger agrees to not keep any pets without obtaining the prior written consent of the Landlord.

12. Access to the Lodger's room

The Landlord agrees not to access the Lodger's room without prior consent with at least 24 hours notice, unless in the case of an emergency.

13. Condition of the property

The Landlord agrees to keep the property reasonably fit for human habitation.

14. Ending the Lodger agreement

The Lodger agreement may be ended by either party giving no less than 28 days written notice.

Lodger's signature: _____   Date: __ / __ / ____

Lodger's full name: _____

Witness's signature: _____   Date: __ / __ / ____

Witness's full name: _____

Landlord's signature: _____   Date: __ / __ / ____

Landlord's full name: _____

Witness's signature: _____   Date: __ / __ / ____

Witness's full name: _____

Inventory

Inventory for (address):_____

Both the Landlord and the Lodger should sign this document. This should be done within the first week of the Lodger moving in. If any extra pages are attached these must be signed by both the Lodger and the Landlord. Keep a copy of this document safely with the lease agreement.

Hall

Lodger's bedroom

Bathroom

Kitchen

Sitting room

Lodger's signature: _____   Date: __ / __ / ____

Landlord's signature: _____   Date: __ / __ / ____

ENGLAND, WALES AND SCOTLAND HOUSEHOLD INVENTORY

Re: (The Property)_____

Living room				
No	Item	Condition	In	Out
1	Armchair	Fair		(condition when leaving)
Etc Etc				
Kitchen				

Bathroom				
Hall				
Bedroom (1-2-3)				
Garden				
Other				

Index

****